CW00665402

LILIAS RIDER HAGGARD
COUNTRYWOMAN

Further details of Poppyland Publishing titles can be found at
www.poppyland.co.uk
*where clicking on the 'Support and Resources' button
will lead to pages specially compiled to support this book*

Join us for more Norfolk and Suffolk stories and background at
www.facebook.com/poppylandpublishing

In memory of my late husband
Peter Beard
1944-2013
With whom I shared many happy times at Ditchingham.

Lilias Rider Haggard Countrywoman

by

Victoria Manthorpe

POPPYLAND
PUBLISHING

Copyright © 2015 Victoria Manthorpe

First published 2015 by Poppyland Publishing, Cromer, NR27 9AN
www.poppyland.co.uk

ISBN 978 1 909796 18 8

All rights reserved. No part of this publication may be reproduced, stored in a retrieval system or transmitted by any means, mechanical, photocopying, recording or otherwise, without the written permission of the publishers.

Designed and typeset in 10.5 on 13.5 pt Gilgamesh
Printed by Lightning Source

Picture credits
Picture credits are included with captions.
The cover of "I Walked by Night" on page 109 and the illustrations on pages 111, 131 and 139 are reproduced by arrangement with the Estate of Edward Seago, represented by Portland Gallery, London.
Front cover painting by William Strang, courtesy Nada Cheyne.
Author's photograph, back cover, by Peter King.

Contents

Acknowledgements

This book has been a long time in the making. I would like to thank especially Nada Cheyne for her generous encouragement, hospitality and friendship over many years. Dorothy Cheyne has been very patient and supportive in providing access to papers and photographs and I am also very grateful to her for checking an early draft.

I would also like to thank:

Diana Athill for her reminiscences of her mother; Peter Boylan for sharing details from his own researches into the Longman papers; Ronald Blyth for early discussion on inter war novelists and writers on country matters; Judith Cheyne, Jonathan Cheyne and Mark Cheyne for their family notes; Mme Una Cochrane for sharing the few surviving photographs of her grandfather Arthur Cochrane.

Erin Gill for sharing her most excellent biographical thesis on Eve Balfour; Russell Gorbell for his reminiscences of his father and the staff at Ditchingham; Mrs Howell for her reminiscences of Margaret Spurrell at Blakeney; Professor Kathryn Hughes of UEA for her mentoring when I began this book as part of a PhD which, alas, I was unable to finish.

Margaret Langley née Sawbridge for her reminiscences of working with Lilias, and of Margaret Spurrell; Margaret Ling for her reminiscences; Caroline MacMillan for information about St Felix School; Giles de la Mare for information on Faber & Faber; Stephanie Norris, professional astrologer for plotting Lilias' horoscope; The late Elizabeth Orr of Didlington House for showing me photographs of Didlingotn Hall, and the Amherst's unimaginably fabulous Egyptian museum; Charlotte Paton for discussing her research on Frederick Rolfe; the Portland Gallery for use of the Edward Seago images; Amanda Shafto for helping with Cochrane family research.

John Smith, clerk of Ditchingham parish council, for allowing me to see the council minutes books; Richard and Jonathan Spurrell for details of the Spurrell family history; Peter Stibbons for publishing this book; Joan Tusting for her recollections; Ann Thwaite for reading a draft manuscript; Adrian Webb for his recollections; Mrs Marie Wilcox for reminiscences of Margaret Spurrell and Spurrell family history; Anne Williamson for sharing Henry Williamson letters and providing a photograph; Professor Tom Williamson of UEA for an initial discussion on agriculture in Norfolk between the wars; Mrs R. Winch of Kettle Hill for recollections of Margaret Spurrell; Rosamund Woodton of Blakeney for recollections of Lilias and use of photographs.

Thanks also to the staff of :

The Country Life Archive; The Devon Record Office; The EDP Archive (Archant); The Norfolk Record Office; The Red Cross Archive and The Bungay Museum.

Introduction

*I hold no brief for a stagnant world. I have seen too much of the bitter
fruit of ignorance and apathy in country places… There is, however,
a breadth, a simplicity and an unhurried dignity about life in these
remote villages, which are even yet untouched by the motor bus,
the cinema, and the summer visitor.*
Lilias Rider Haggard, Introduction to
I Walked by Night (1935)

Lilias Rider Haggard was a writer of country matters: nature, rural lore, rural crafts, local and family history. Her best known works are two poignant reminiscences that she edited: *I Walked by Night* (1935) and *The Rabbit Skin Cap* (1939). Her writing was contexted in a particular time and place and therefore it is best understood in the light of who she was, of her life story. This study of Lilias Rider Haggard is set in upper class, conservative society as British Imperialism declined. The original source material, that includes over three hundred unpublished letters, manuscripts and photograph albums, shows her preoccupations to be prescribed by family life.

As a young child Lilias was camera shy. Of the many photographs in which she figures only a few show her standing still or face on. Except in studio portraits she turned hurriedly away from the shutter's gaze leaving little more than a smudge in the group pictures of her family. Instinctively she did not care to be seen. Instead she turned her attention to the natural world — to animals and landscape — and merged herself into it. Landscape can be kind to those who seek camouflage. In between the shifting shadows on a hillside, in the dense undergrowth,

Young Lilias with a family group at Ditchingham, typically turning away from the camera. Cheyne Collection.

Lilias : the middle-aged countrywoman.
Cheyne Collection.

among the complex outlines of a stand of trees, or under the uneven surface of moving water - in all these changing natural features many feelings may be hidden.

In the 1940s and 1950s Lilias Rider Haggard was a familiar middle-aged figure in Norfolk — at parish council meetings, on county council committees, at school prize-givings, agricultural shows, fêtes and Women's Institute events. Of average height — perhaps five foot six inches or five foot seven inches, she was full-bosomed in twinsets, tweed skirts and sensible country shoes. When not on parade she could be seen in an old Barbour coat and Wellington boots. She had a fair complexion and, even in middle age, had golden hair that did not fade or grey — a distinctive feature inherited from her mother's family, the Margitsons. Her high cheekbones and greenish, vulpine eyes came via the Haggards from the Meybohms, her wealthy Russian Jewish ancestors. She was unmistakably of the gentry with a cut-glass voice, stylish motor cars and fur coats. She was said to have "no side" because she could speak with anyone on equal terms as long as she shared their interests. That was an important caveat because what interested her were country matters: farming, dogs, ornithology, wildlife and gardens. Having "no side" did not mean that she was not fully aware of class and her superior place in the structure. In fact she was automatically deferred to by the lower orders. She had no time for wimps: an attitude that was common amongst the upper classes but which could seem quite harsh to sensitive souls and small children. She was, nevertheless, very helpful and kind in practical ways to the many members of her large circle of family and friends. All the "county" people, the local landed families and their friends, knew her socially; she was part of their landscape. Yet, being part of the landscape meant that she was not always seen for herself and her personal and emotional life remained obscure.

Lilias was born, lived and died at Ditchingham, a village in the Waveney Valley, close to the market town of Bungay on the border between Norfolk and Suffolk. Location is central to her story. The countryside is not a natural formation but man-made over centuries. Ditchingham had been shaped at least as far back as the Romans when they grew grapes along what are still known as the Vineyard Hills.

In *Keywords: A Vocabulary of Culture and Society* (1976) Raymond Williams, an academic cultural theorist, called "nature", "perhaps the most complex word in the language". According to Williams the meaning of "nature" may mean the Goddess herself but since the eighteenth century has also meant the countryside and "unspoiled places". Since Darwin's *On the Origin of the Species* (1869) "nature" has also included the possible connotations of survival, evolution and the selective breeder. All these usages come into play in twentieth century texts on rural and country matters, especially in the period between the World Wars. But it is as well to remember also that the word "country" derives from an old French adjective for the feminine which in turn comes from the Latin "*contra*" or against – lying opposite against or facing.[1]

George Orwell in his essay "Inside the Whale" called the preoccupation with country themes in poetry between 1910 and 1925 the snobbism of the rentier-professional class who had lost touch with farming. This was not the case with Lilias. Her books emerge from her knowledge of landscape, of rural life and from the force field of her relationship with her father and his writing. The recent resurgence of nature writing in the twenty-first century includes new thematic approaches and an ecological emphasis. Discovering and recognizing the roots of these contemporary books in the political and cultural developments in the twentieth century is a core strand of this biography.

There was only ever one important man in Lilias' life: her father, Sir Henry Rider Haggard. As a world-famous and prolific author of adventure stories and romances, he gave Lilias a passport to recognition but he also cast a long shadow over her own life and work. With a handful of extraordinary exceptions, including *King Solomon's Mines* and *She*, Rider Haggard's 58 novels and his many political reports and studies have been long-forgotten. Despite his two knighthoods, he died a disappointed man. He did not feel that he had been able to contribute to public life in the way that he would have wished. All his life he chased wealth to the detriment of his talents and his higher self. It was a pattern set in boyhood to try to disprove his father's low opinion of his abilities and he took on the financial responsibility for several of his less successful brothers and their many children. His slip-shod writing style, his refusal to pay due homage to his generous creative muse, and the irrevocable change in attitudes to British imperialism have pushed

[1]   R. J. White, *The Conservative Tradition* (London: Nicholas Kaye 1950), 71.

his work into the backwaters of English cultural history. Yet, even though the literati and academics may disdain him, Rider Haggard's intuitive story-telling skills inspired generations of writers. Many a fine author, from Graham Greene to William Golding[2], has paid homage to boyhood inspiration from reading Rider Haggard.

For Rider fiction was how he made his living and he had a second, and to him more worthy, string to his bow: his knowledge and study of agriculture. At the turn of the twentieth century, during a desperate recession caused by poor harvests and cheap grain from the American and Canadian prairies, he diverted his energies from writing novels to produce his own substantial studies: *A Farmer's Year* (1899); *Rural England* (1902); and *The Poor and the Land* (1905). These are in the tradition of William Cobbett and Thomas Tusser; they are factual surveys deliberately written to influence political policy and focus on the facts and figures of farming, but they contain elements common to Virgil's *Georgics* — advice and description of farming methods.

In his novels Rider Haggard gave landscape mythic and religious qualities but in his non-fiction studies of agriculture he organised, formalised, subdued and capitalized upon it. In neither case was he sentimental about the countryside or agriculture. "Nature" was unforgiving but there was a strong spirituality in his interpretation: ignore the land at your peril. Rider Haggard's appraisals contribute to the history of agricultural practice and provide a contemporary social commentary, albeit largely from the farmer's point of view.

Lilias had none of her father's biblical rhetoric or radical political views and her own writing derives more from the lyrical observations of Richard Jefferies (1848-1887) than from Cobbett or Young. Lilias was part of a conservative trend that identified the land as sacred. Similar pagan themes had been emerging in Europe, particularly in Germany, for several decades and are connected to the political discussions of the 1930s. However, from the twenty-first century perspective, we see more clearly what havoc industrialisation has wrought to the earth's ecosystems, and some of the reactionary writers of the 1930s look more like prophets. Particularly interesting are figures of the political right whose ideology of the land led to experiments in organic farming, an area explored by Richard Griffith in his book *Fellow Travellers of the Right*.

Lilias began writing articles on historical and country subjects in 1929 for national and regional newspapers. Her diary of "A Country Woman's Week" first appeared in the *Eastern Daily Press* in 1936 followed by her regular "Countrywoman" columns. Because of the size of Norfolk and the long distances

[2]   In *An Egyptian Journal*, Golding wrote "But on Haggard I would spend my all, walk miles for one of his books, read and reread without end." Page 9. Faber & Faber London: 1985.

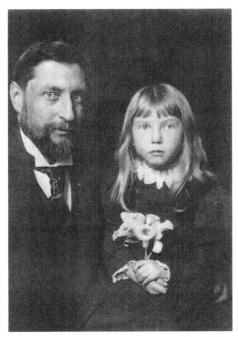

H. Rider Haggard with his young daughter Lilias 1890s. Cheyne Collection.

between towns, the *Eastern Daily Press* (known locally as the EDP) was more than a local newspaper, it was an institution that kept all the far-flung agricultural communities informed and in contact. Lilias' columns became part of that Norfolk identity.

During the second World War Lilias' columns took on a new tone. They were inevitably more serious and are a stark record of how the war effort impacted at a parochial level. Nostalgia, a yearning for home, must by definition involve separation so that in some ways the war was a gift to Lilias' style of writing. By stimulating an interest in country crafts and vanishing customs she was able to establish an historical authority for "home". Because that "home", Norfolk, was more locally defined than the nation of England she was able to avoid domestic political issues while at the same time inviting an even deeper loyalty to place.

From our stand point in a democratic age it may seem odd that a member of the gentry was recognized as having a collective voice. The effect of some recent books such as *The Remains of the Day* has been to imply that the upper classes were inclined, as a group, to sympathise with Fascism. As we shall see, there were indeed some notable individual examples of this in Norfolk, but more usually in landed and aristocratic families every able-bodied male joined one of the armed services in the battle against Fascism and the women supported the effort either in the women's forces or at home. Soon after the war, the author and critic, R.H. Mottram was able to sum up the apparent anomaly of her wide appeal in his review for the *Observer* of a collection of Lilias' work in a *Norfolk Notebook*.

Across the book falls the shadow of Munich and after. Then something happens that cannot be explained to any inhabitant of Europe. All that leisured class which Miss Rider Haggard represents, unorganised and unwillingly heaved itself up, Norfolk became again the place that sent its ships to the Armada and welcomed Nelson home. Trenches were dug, noncombatants evacuated, food hoarded, ARP posts manned. For behind all this interest in "a bundle of little silver birches to plant along the meadow below the wood" is something very resilient, a habit of life less interrupted, better based than most national habits. One feels that it is not likely to succumb to the many troubles of the moment.[3]

Mottram identified a factor in national life without which the work of Lilias Rider Haggard could be dismissed as just so many more diary entries from an Edwardian lady. It was her steady dedication to observing nature and recording the daily round, the continuity of country life that had and has social and national value.

Equally important in terms of cultural history is to see in Lilias' life the twentieth century struggle for feminine identity in a patriarchal society. On the one hand she was just a single example of a woman caught in masculine identification; on the other, her dilemma is highly significant in that her father had given birth to *She*, a powerful archetype of repressed femininity. It is not apparent that he understood the phenomenon himself leave alone the effects on his daughter and her relationships.

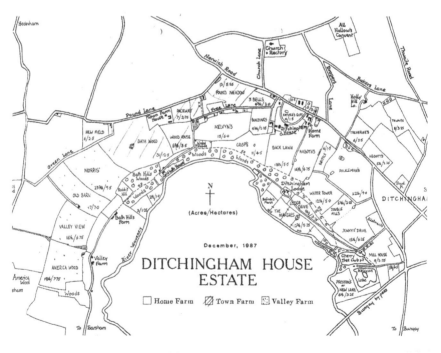

A map of the Ditchingham House estate.

3   Quoted on the dust jacket, *Norfolk Notebook,* (London: Faber, 1950).

The Children of William and Ella Haggard of Bradenham Hall, Norfolk

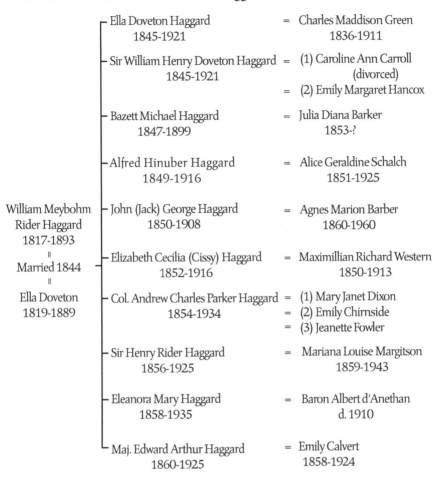

William Meybohm
Rider Haggard
1817-1893
‖
Married 1844
‖
Ella Doveton
1819-1889

- Ella Doveton Haggard
  1845-1921
  = Charles Maddison Green
  1836-1911

- Sir William Henry Doveton Haggard =
  1845-1921
  (1) Caroline Ann Carroll
  (divorced)
  = (2) Emily Margaret Hancox

- Bazett Michael Haggard
  1847-1899
  = Julia Diana Barker
  1853-?

- Alfred Hinuber Haggard
  1849-1916
  = Alice Geraldine Schalch
  1851-1925

- John (Jack) George Haggard
  1850-1908
  = Agnes Marion Barber
  1860-1960

- Elizabeth Cecilia (Cissy) Haggard
  1852-1916
  = Maximillian Richard Western
  1850-1913

- Col. Andrew Charles Parker Haggard =
  1854-1934
  (1) Mary Janet Dixon
  = (2) Emily Chirnside
  = (3) Jeanette Fowler

- Sir Henry Rider Haggard
  1856-1925
  = Mariana Louise Margitson
  1859-1943

- Eleanora Mary Haggard
  1858-1935
  = Baron Albert d'Anethan
  d. 1910

- Maj. Edward Arthur Haggard
  1860-1925
  = Emily Calvert
  1858-1924

The Children of Rider and Louisa Haggard

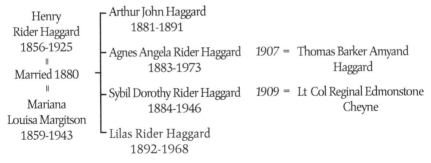

Henry
Rider Haggard
1856-1925
‖
Married 1880
‖
Mariana
Louisa Margitson
1859-1943

- Arthur John Haggard
  1881-1891

- Agnes Angela Rider Haggard   1907 = Thomas Barker Amyand
  1883-1973   Haggard

- Sybil Dorothy Rider Haggard   1909 = Lt Col Reginal Edmonstone
  1884-1946   Cheyne

- Lilas Rider Haggard
  1892-1968

Lilias Rider Haggard and two of her dogs.
Cheyne Collection.

I

The Garden at Ditchingham

Lilias was born into a winter landscape. It was December 9th 1892 and snow lay on the ground. The years of both the century and the Victorian epoch were waning. Within the Haggard family Lilias arrived into a story that was already told. Her father, Rider, had married an heiress, Louisa Margitson (known as Louie) who owned a small estate in south Norfolk. They had started married life in Africa where they intended to settle and where their son and heir was born. Political uncertainty prompted their return to England where they added to their family with two little girls. Trained as a lawyer, Rider had serious aspirations to public life but he had made his name and his fortune as a writer of adventure stories for boys; their prospects looked assured. Then early in 1891, while Rider and Louie were abroad, their son had died of a sudden illness. His death shook their marriage to its foundations and left Rider's ambitions adrift. What possible new thing could Lilias bring to this family's narrative?

Yet, as with every new birth, there was a hope of Eden.

When Lilias was born Rider was, at the age of thirty-six, in his prime. He was the eighth of ten children: seven brothers and three sisters, born in the mid-nineteenth century. They were already a legend to themselves and some of them were also launched on the world stage. Their temperaments ranged from nervous to excitable, from adventurous to impetuous and from highly-sexed to neurotic. Their father William Haggard, the squire of West Bradenham Hall near Swaffham in Norfolk, had Nordic, Jewish, Slavic and French

Mariana Louisa Haggard née Margitson – handsome and stylish in a London studio portrait.
Cheyne Collection.

Huguenot blood coursing through his English veins. William Haggard's paternal ancestry was rooted into several centuries of very substantial merchants from Hertfordshire who had arrived in Norfolk early in the nineteenth century.

William Haggard was virile, dynastic and shrewd; according to Rider he ruled Bradenham like a king. Rider also said he never met anyone who bore the least resemblance to his father. He taught his sons to shout loud enough to be heard across his fields and it was said that when they visited Norwich he could shout from the central market place and gather them all in from their various destinations. When they were young, he would fling gold coins down the staircase of the Hall for them to scramble after: for better and for worse, it created a pattern for their

William Meybohm Rider Haggard Esquire, Justice of the Peace, Deputy Lieutenant of the County and for 36 years Chairman of the Quarter Sessions for the county of Norfolk. Cheyne Collection.

lives. With dazzling charm and loud voices they scrambled and shouted their way around the world. When they left home the Squire persisted in commanding their careers and marriages, sometimes with disastrous results; yet with all his domineering ways, he was passionate and warm. William Haggard had died earlier in the same year that Lilias was born.

Rider's mother, Ella Doveton, had brought an ancestry of wealthy colonial grandees to the family tree. She also brought refinement, knowledge of India and Egypt, a strong literary taste and some talent for verse. Unlike her husband, Mrs Haggard spoke with a quiet voice and everyone listened. Rider adored her. However, her poems, which include strong imagery and savage descriptions of the Indian mutiny, suggest that she may have been quiet but not necessarily gentle in spirit. She had died three years previously, on the exact day of Lilias' birth, and almost to the same early morning hour.

The Haggards had loosed their mercantile moorings when they aspired to the status of landed gentry and thereafter their fortune was subject to the ebb and flow of agricultural tides. When facing financial straits William Haggard would decamp temporarily and take the family to Europe and cheaper living. A major slump in the 1870s together with a surge of imperial expansion led the boys to seek their fortunes overseas. William (Will), the eldest son, had been sent to Winchester College and entered the *Corps Diplomatique* from which superior vantage point, eventually as an ambassador, he was able to help his brothers from time to time. Unfortunately, none of the rest was content with the status of a "younger son", who might perhaps have accepted the income and rank of a provincial professional; they all desired the prominence of gentry. The Indian Civil Service claimed Alfred until he disagreed with imperial policies and governance-by-fear and came home in disgrace. He took up Positivism, a philosophy of science based entirely on empiricism. Bazett went into law until financial failure and alcoholism drove him into minor consular service in Samoa where he kept company with Robert Louis Stevenson and his household. Jack was sent as a carrot-headed boy into the Royal Navy, which he loathed from the beginning and throughout his service that began in the Nicobar Islands and included the March to Magdala in the Abyssinian Campaign, Mexico and Siam. Later Will found him minor consular posts initially in Lamu and Madagascar before he was moved on to Brest, Florence and southern Spain. Andrew was commissioned into the King's Own Scottish Borderers serving with distinction in Egypt and the Sudan alongside heroic soldiers of the period — William Butler, Herbert Kitchener and Redvers Buller.[1] Later he did a stint in India but retired early and impecuniously and was always on the *qui vive* until he made an advantageous marriage. Rider was sent out to South Africa as a factotum to a Norfolk neighbour, Henry Bulwer, on his mission to annexe the Transvaal.[2] In his autobiography Rider attributed the arrangement to his father but contemporary letters show that it was his mother who organised the posting. After a shaky start Rider did well as a law clerk to Judge Kotzé and then decided to try his luck at farming with his friend and business partner Arthur Cochrane, a relative of the then famous adventurer Thomas Cochrane, 10th Earl of Dundonald.[3] It was in the midst of this shaky venture that he came home and courted Louisa Margitson and, upon marrying her, took her back to Africa where their first child was born. The first Boer War of 1881 put paid to Rider's hopes of a colonial life and they returned reluctantly to England where he read for the bar. The youngest Haggard brother, Edward, joined the Shropshire regiment and became a career soldier.

Of the girls, the eldest, Ella was the most stable. Married to a patient and able clergyman, Charles Maddison Green, vicar of Lyonshall near Ledbury in

---

[1]   They became, respectively, General Sir William Butler, Field Marshall Lord Kitchener and General Sir Redvers Buller.
[2]   The Bulwer family came from Heydon in north Norfolk.
[3]   His naval exploits inspired the writers C.S. Forester and Patrick O'Brian.

Herefordshire, she provided a second heartland for the family. Her husband was often called upon to disentangle the family embarrassments. Elizabeth Cecilia, known as Cissie, showed signs of what was then thought of as mental instability (or hysteria) and was married off with dispatch to an unattractive-looking civil engineer. She bore four daughters in as many years, succumbed to what may have been anorexia and schizophrenia and suffered a life-long incarceration in St Andrew's Hospital near Northampton. A story survives in Norfolk that it was one of her diaries that provided the inspiration for L.P. Hartley's novel of illicit love *The Go-Between*.

Rider's youngest sister, Eleanora, was what might best be described as "a character". Her marriage to a rotund Belgian diplomat was viewed with ribald derision by her brothers who thought she would have little pleasure from the union. There were no children and she matured into an exaggerated doyenne and occasional authoress.

The Haggards were great letter writers, scrawling vigorously and spontaneously from every corner of the Empire. By this process they had been writing their family saga for many years and because so many of the letters were kept, at least until after World War II, it was a saga that was available within the family and for the next generation of numerous cousins — and the stories were repeated and exchanged. They quarrelled amongst themselves, particularly over inheritances and perceived slights, but remained fixedly loyal within the family firmament, remembering each others' birthdays and staying in each others houses at home and abroad. Socially, they moved exclusively within an upper middle class elite in which families always had connection with or knowledge of each other; this elite was also the ruling class of Empire and was recognizable in Cairo or Calcutta, Cape Town or Hong Kong.

For the Haggards their sense of home and of Englishness was acute because, although they loved to travel, they all suffered from home-sickness. Their many moves and years spent abroad produced nostalgia. Home, normally the place where you are, was defined by not being there — paradise lost.

Although only a small fraction of their correspondence survives, it is still a very significant collection that highlights many of the most dramatic and important incidents in their lives. Jack's letters from his naval days provided many of the incidents that Rider was later able to use in his novels.[4] Several of the siblings aspired to publication. Andrew and Edward wrote novels; Andrew also wrote histories of France and biographies. Eleanora wrote novels and her memoirs of Japan. Alfred wrote political pamphlets. It fell to Rider to make his name and his living as an author. While he struggled with the law, Rider had written two

---

[4]   See Victoria Manthorpe, *Children of the Empire* (London: Gollancz, 1996).

romantic novels: *Dawn* and *The Witch's Head*. Fame came upon him suddenly in 1885 with his third effort, this time an adventure aimed at boys. Cassell promoted *King Solomon's Mines* on London billboards and omnibuses as THE GREATEST STORY EVER TOLD. It was the first adventure story of Africa, it coincided fortuitously with the development of the fabulous Kimberley diamond mines, it was a quest that appealed to all ages, it had an accessible, untutored, yarning style with many flashes of humour and it introduced a not-too-brave, not-too-noble but decent sort of chap, Allan Quatermain, as its hero. Rider followed that success with three more sensational books, *She*, *Jess* and *Allan Quatermain*, before he settled down to steady annual production of popular adventures and romances that sustained his reputation and a very comfortable standard of living.

These were the characters and events in the Haggard drama.

In the decade of the 1890s the century itself was spent, having delivered its industrial vitality. Even the story of Empire was nearly over (although few recognised it yet), while Europe was producing a last vivid show of neo-Romantic fireworks. Rural life in the Waveney Valley, on the border between south Norfolk and north Suffolk, had not changed much since the Margitsons arrived in the eighteenth century; nevertheless the decadent breezes of *fin de siècle* with its intimations of the occult, fascination with the dead and fears of racial degeneration did still blow across the mental landscape of its educated inhabitants.

There was no longer a farm in Africa. Rider and his partners had sold it in 1883. His hopes for a life as a colonial settler away from the social rigidity of Victorian society were a thing of the past. *King Solomon's Mines* had yielded its bounty but the treasure hunting was not quite over. In 1891 he and Louie became involved in an escapade inspired directly by a gentleman adventurer called John Gladwyn Jebb.

Jebb had had a tough upbringing, spent some time in the army in India, and risked his insufficient private income on a variety of wild business ventures. When Rider and Louie met Jebb and his wife at a dinner party in London he was concerned with Mexican silver mines. Rider was mesmerised by Jebb's combination of fearless enterprise and a deeply sensitive and psychic nature.[5] It was to be a fateful association.

Rider and Louie accepted the Jebbs' invitation to join them after their return to Mexico City. They may have seen it as a chance to be an adventurous couple again. They left their children (Jock aged 9, Angie aged 6 and Dolly, 5) first with one of Louie's aunts and then with two sets of friends: Mr and Mrs Edmund

5   Mrs John Beveridge Gladwyn Jebb, *A Strange Career; life and adventures of John Gladwyn Jebb* (Boston: Roberts Brothers, 1895).

Gosse and Mr and Mrs Barrington Foote. Rider had a premonition that he would not see his son again but thought his own life was the one in danger. Rider and Louie sailed from Liverpool to New York and then travelled by train through what was still the Wild West and crossed the border to Mexico. They were in search of a new story for Rider and for the gold that Cortez supposedly flung down the shaft of a silver mine in his flight from the vengeance of the Incas. But gold and silver and the dreams of Cortez were to slide beyond their grasp.

Rider and Louie had barely arrived in Mexico City before they received a wire telling them the impossibly dreadful news that their little boy Jock had died suddenly. Jock had developed measles soon after his parents left but this illness had covered other more serious symptoms. The autopsy revealed an ulcer of long-standing and the collapse of a lung with pleurisy. With one nine-year -old boy, badly diagnosed, perhaps carelessly nursed, Rider's dynastic expectations also died. The funeral service and burial took place in the absence of his parents with family members standing in. The restless, reckless dreams of youth and confidence were over. A world of patriarchal expectation lay with a small boy cold in his Ditchingham grave.

Beyond those expectations and ambitions, the grief was acute. Rider succumbed to nervous shock. In an attempt to aid his recovery by distraction the kindly Gladwyn Jebb persuaded him to make the journey through the mountains to see the remains of the Aztec cities and the mines. Louie, no less devastated, had iron self-control and stayed with Mrs Jebb in Mexico City pacing the verandas. In the late spring they came home to their little girls and the little grave. All Jock's toys and clothes were locked away in his room never to be opened and Rider forbade even mention of his name. The suppression was absolute.

Rider became ill with influenza, headaches, digestive problems and depression. He gave up his house in Redcliffe Square in London and turned away from his usual pursuits and from his friends. He could not physically write but he still needed to make a living; he hired a secretary Ida Hector to take dictation.[6] He gave himself up to a morose grief.

The next spring Louie and Rider conceived another child. Rider was pleased but to Louie, according to Lilias, "the prospect of another child . . . was not welcome".[7] It would mean a return to the cares and ties of the nursery: the long nights, the worries and fretting, the many life-threatening childhood illnesses

---

[6]   Ida Hector was the daughter of the Irish novelist and hymn writer Mrs Annie Hector who wrote under the pseudonym Mrs Alexander. See Chapter 16 of *The Days of My Life*. Mrs Hector's father was a Norfolk land agent – research from D.S. Higgins Rider Haggard, *The Great Storyteller*, page 152 and Peter Beresford Ellis, *A Voice from the Infinite*.

[7]   LRH, *The Cloak that I Left*, 158.

that were the norm of the time and have only quite recently in the late twentieth century been banished by inoculations. Still, the child would be a replacement for the lost son; perhaps they could recover the planned narrative.

Lilias arrived early in the dark early morning hours of December 9th 1892.[8] The child was shockingly not male but a little girl. Rider's relatives hurried to write letters of commiseration. But after the initial disappointment Rider, for reasons that will emerge, accepted the new order: the female child. He repulsed the pity and celebrated new life. He took to the new baby in a very modern way and when Louie grew tired in the evenings, Rider would take the baby and nurse her over his shoulder as he dictated the *People of the Mist* and revised *Montezuma's Daughter* — the latter a novel written out of his Mexican travels. His health began to improve.

There is no account of Lilias' experience of her earliest years with her family but she later recalled a disturbing memory of childhood dreams:

> I seemed to be cast off from the earth altogether, and falling — falling — through illimitable space and fathomless darkness, illumined only by vast iridescent bubbles swelling and shrinking like great worlds reeling through blackness, I was lost, lost forever, never to regain my small comfortable body, left behind in a tiny vanished universe, until I was caught, and held, and pulled back — by the lighting of a candle. I can still see the last of those immense floating bubble worlds dissolving before the light of that small flame.
>
> I believe my elders, distressed by these night terrors, at last asked the doctor what could be the cause of them, to receive the prosaic reply that I was cutting a very large set of back teeth. Be that as it may, I had lost a good many of those teeth before I lost my nightmares.[9]

In her dream Lilias had lost her connection with her body. One may speculate, and it is speculation, that the missing link was the mothering element. Louie, independent and self-contained, may not have responded emotionally to this new being who had joined her family. How and when Lilias became aware of the brother she had been conceived to replace is not known.

Ditchingham House sat in ten acres of gardens, shrubberies, tennis courts and stables. Louie's grandfather had arranged for the main Bungay to Norwich road to be moved away from the front drive so that he could create a substantial front lawn. The three-storey house was brick with large bay windows on two sides and a

8   When the sun was in Sagittarius and the Moon in Leo and most probably Scorpio rising. Lilias' horoscope was plotted by astrologer Stephanie Norris in 2014.
9   Article in the *Eastern Daily Press* January 29th 1955.

pitched roof covered in yellow lichen. Rider had turned the upstairs billiard room with its wide casement windows into his study overlooking the back gardens and he embarked on a long programme of alterations in the rest of the house, introducing extensive oak panelling, doors and fittings.

Lilias shared a nursery with her older sisters. To escape the day-to-day trials of child-raising Louie brought her twin spinster relatives, Cousin Rose and Cousin Lily Hildyard, to attend to the young child. Rose and Lily were very kind and very genteel but neither worldly nor clever. Many years later Lilias dramatised them as hopelessly ineffectual twins "Rosemary" and "Lavender" who were unable to find their train tickets.[10]

The Ditchingham day began with family prayers with Rider reading from the Bible followed by breakfast. Lilias' sisters were too much older to be her playmates in her nursery days and as soon as she was old enough she was turned out into the garden to play. The gardens were not uninhabited: gardeners and farm workers were all about. There was wildlife aplenty and in this outdoor domestic sphere Rider was most active. On his return from Mexico he had found that gardening was one of the few activities that could divert him from his grief and he set about developing the gardens surrounding the house. He had brought

Ditchingham House faces on to the east side of the Norwich road near Bungay.
Cheyne Collection.

[10]   LRH, *A Country Notebook* column in the *Eastern Daily Press,* cutting undated but during the 1941 North Africa Campaign of World War II..

Angie and Dolly with baby Lilias, probably 1893. Cheyne Collection.

back exotic plants for which he built heated greenhouses — a fig and tomato house, a peach house and both a cool and a hot orchid house — in which he spent hours propagating and cherishing his beloved fruits and blooms. Over a period of time he established more than an acre of flower garden and he never went out without a bloom in the buttonhole of his lapel. A new three-quarter-acre kitchen garden supplied the house with vegetables and there was a lily pond, a water garden, shrubberies and more than three hundred fruit trees as well as tennis and

The long and bounteous rose border at Ditchingham with a figure leaning out of Riders' study window, probably Miss Hector. From A Gardener's Year, *page 232.*

croquet lawns. Louie was a keen and competitive croquet player.

Gardening was a relatively new subject for books and Rider plunged in with a detailed but lively monthly account of his gardens during 1903, published in 1904 as *A Gardener's Year*, which he dedicated to one of his Bungay neighbours, Mrs Robert Mann. *A Gardener's Year* reveals many domestic arrangements as well as Rider's deep involvement in the running of his estate and his close interest and observation of the natural world; among these good sensible facts are occasional reflections about the nature of life. All of these interests were absorbed by Lilias.

The soil was stiff loam upon blue clay which needed pick axes to shift it and when he had first come to Ditchingham the gardens had been managed by one man and a boy. But as Rider developed its complexity it required the attention of a gardener (Mason) and a boy (Charles), both full time, and the part time help of a household servant who cleaned knives and boots and brought in the coal (Freaks) and an occasional labouring man (Knowles) for heavy work. This was in addition to Rider himself.

One of the most outstanding qualities of *A Gardener's Year* is the author's personal and practical involvement. He concerned himself with every aspect of the work: the layout of beds and lawns; the digging of ponds; the designs of the hot houses; the procuring of stock and plants; the clearing of drains and gutters.

When at home he made a daily inspection of his gardens and rolled up his sleeves to help with the work, for example in February 1903:

> For two days in the middle of the week all hands, excepting
> Knowles, who was engaged in wheeling the turf mould to the
> Cucumber-frame and shovelling it on to the top of the manure,
> were hard at work building our new Rockery, which I think ought
> really to prove a great success. First of all we cut a path through

A map of the garden from A Gardener's Year.

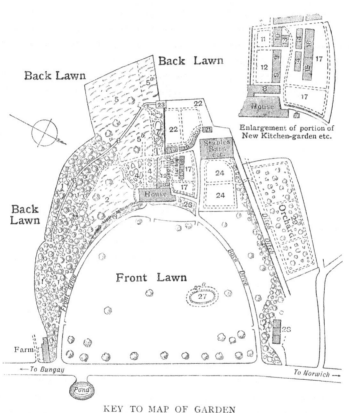

KEY TO MAP OF GARDEN

1 Shrubbery	converted into Mush-	19 Peach-house
2 Old Lawn	room-house, &c.	20 Fig and Tomato-house
3 Bank with Yew Fence on	9 Greenhouses	21 Old Dog-kennel
top	10 Cold Orchid-house	22 Old Kitchen Garden
4 Flower-garden with orna-	11 Flower Bed	23 Pond recently enlarged
mental beds	12 Old Vinery-border	24 Stable Garden
4a Open Flower-border	13 Boiler and old Mushroom-	25 Rubbish Yard
5 Tennis Lawn	houses (now Potting-	26 Shrubbery with Dog-kennel
5a New addition	shed)	27 Water Garden
5b Grass	14 Pits	27a New Pond Border
6 Sunk Walk	15 Warm Orchid-house	28 Cottages with Shrubbery
7 Elm-tree Garden with old	16 Cool Orchid-house	29 Orchard
Yew Fence	17 New Kitchen Garden	= = = = = Garden Paths
8 Old Potting-shed, &c., now	18 Intermediate-house	

> the middle of the little piece of land. Our method of making this
> and the other narrow paths in the Elm-tree garden is simple,
> but, where there is not much heavy wheeling to be done, fairly
> effective. Also it is cheap. We get some marl from a pit on the
> farm, and, since all our hard stuff is wanted for the Orchard road
> and footways, lay it direct onto the clay bed. Then we bring sand
> from another pit and spread it thickly over the marl, to which it
> clings. A path thus formed will be found to answer all ordinary
> purposes, and if the sand is deep enough and the subsoil not too
> wet it does not stick to the feet even in the rain.[11]

For such a practical man an entry from March shows his surprising soft-heartedness and his preoccupation with the nature of mortality. They had had trouble with mice eating crocus bulbs but when he found one in a trap he could not bring himself to drown it but went out of his way to release it in a field. Formal pheasant shoots were part of the social calendar for the gentry at Ditchingham but Rider gave up shooting as he had given up riding to hounds.

Rider only mentions Lilias twice in *A Gardener's Year*, but the affection is evident, first in March:

> I walked on the Bath or Vineyard hills that afternoon, an
> extraordinarily sheltered spot facing south, and protected by its
> steep bank, eighty or ninety feet in depth, crested as it is with fir
> and other trees, from every breath of north and easterly winds.
> Here things are getting very forward, and my little girl, who was
> with me, gathered quite a nice posy of Primroses and Violets.[12]

Second, in December in relation to a frog that needs releasing from the Cool Orchid House: "... I think that it was placed there by my little girl two or three years ago. "[13]

Rider's humanity is also markedly sensitive in relation to his household servants:

> I think, however, that in gardening, as in other trades, and
> more so than in many, the master makes the man. It is not in
> the grandest places where most money is spent that the best
> gardeners are always found, but rather, I believe, in those where
> the employer takes a lively, personal interest in what goes on
> from day to day, and is in constant consultation with his servant,
> or servants, how to attain the greatest measure of success of
> which his means and circumstances admit.[14]

[11] HRH, *A Gardener's Year,* (London: Longmans, Green, and Co., 1903), 73.
[12] Ibid, 101.
[13] Ibid, 387.
[14] Ibid, 195.

The stubbornness and idiosyncrasy of the East Anglian country people was something with which Rider was fully familiar since his boyhood at Bradenham. They had their own ways and Rider told amusing anecdotes about how the labourers prevailed over their squire and sometimes proved him foolish as well.

The pattern of daily life can also be glimpsed from *A Gardener's Year*. In the morning much of Rider's time was spent tending his garden and farms, the afternoon and some evenings were devoted to dictating his novels to Miss Hector. He frequently travelled up to London on his own for business and to attend plant auctions. In the summer months he showed his orchids at Norwich flower shows. Despite the company of his two dogs and his gardeners there is an impression of a solitary life. The companionship of his "little girl" was very welcome. He took humorous pleasure in the idiosyncrasies of his servants:

> I remember that when I first began to send Orchids to these shows, my late old gardener, who we will call "A", objected. He was not accustomed to that kind of thing, and appeared to have no rooted confidence in the judges, whom so many of his class believed to be influenced by considerations other than those of the merits of the exhibits. At length he yielded, to my arguments, adding, "Well, I daresay, like other gentlemen, *yew [sic] would like to see your name in print for once.*" For such he conceived to be the real object of this new departure! I must say that it struck me as strange that he should have been in my service for nearly twenty years and yet remain unaware that my name *had* appeared in print — occasionally.[15]

Rider's attitude to women also emerges from the pages of *A Gardener's Year*. This anecdote about gardener "A" illustrates the teasing banter and humorous atmosphere which was prevalent at Ditchingham:

> "A." was no believer in the other sex, whom he looked on as utterly irresponsible creatures, with pronounced evil tendencies, who picked his flowers, and were everlastingly clamouring for vegetables that he had forgotten to grow. Still, he recognised that such beings were entitled to the pity of their superiors, although, certainly in his case, that pity was not akin to love. Some female delinquency was under discussion, when suddenly he drew himself up and, waving an empty flower-pot, enunciated an aphorism that has become famous in certain local circles.
>
> "They can't think like we; I say them there womens can't think,

---

15   Ibid, 223.

but don't *yew*[sic] be hard on "em" — a pause, then, with a burst
of conviction — "*They does their best po'r things!*"

Somehow this immortal saying, when repeated in argument,
always produces irritation, even among those classes of the "po'r
things" who consider themselves to be endowed with powers of
reflection.[16]

Rider himself had, for the times, a more enlightened attitude to women as
evidenced from his report on a visit to a farm at Colne Engaine (ten miles north
west of Colchester) in Essex managed by a woman for her father:

This farm, with its able and intelligent manager, who knows
every detail of its working, and even pays the men herself; its
clean dairy, where a lady pupil with a cheerful countenance
was cleansing the place after butter-making; its fruit Orchards;
its fowls fattening in coops; and its charming Homestead, was
indeed a pleasant place to visit. Why, I wonder, do not more
ladies learn the practical management of land, to which, I am
sure many of them are quite as competent, indeed, more so, than
the ordinary hide-bound, tenant-farmer.[17]

Women are, I'm glad to say, taking to gardening in increasing
numbers, and can receive education in that art at various
colleges.[18]

*The Elm Tree Garden at Ditchingham showing the dense
and complex spaces Rider created. From* A Gardener's
Year *page 289.*

During her early years Lilias
was educated at home, although
not very effectively as she was to
find out when she finally went
to a school. Her world only
extended beyond Ditchingham
to other places which her family
might visit. Her earliest letters
sent by her to her occasionally-
absent parents describe fossils,
the behaviour of the dogs,
breeding pigeons, trying to
tame a bat from instructions in
a book, anticipating catching

[16]   Ibid, 223/4.
[17]   Ibid, 128.
[18]   Ibid,129.

harvest mice for pets from a haystack, and putting up nesting boxes for wild birds which again she identified from a book. She seems to have had encouragement in consulting bird books from her mother who in other ways was a distant figure, seldom referred to in Lilias' later writings. One letter sent to her mother while the latter was in London is signed charmingly but what could be interpreted as a little needy ... your very loving little daughter Lilias."

Describing her childhood when she was an adult she recalled:

> I was clad in an enveloping blue overall (showing a bright patch at the bottom where the hem had been let down), and turned out into the garden. The elders knew nothing of what filled my days; of the adventures in the farm and shrubbery, of the fairy world encircled by the shade of a single beech with the rain-filled cranny in its roots which was the queen's bath.

> ... Of the animal cemetery under the laurels with headstones of broken slate, and the very smelly and imperfectly buried remains. So active did this passion become that a positive body-snatching of corpses became the rage between me and two companions of the moment. No matter what stage of decomposition they had reached they were treasure trove, fodder for another tomb. This lasted until the skull collection reigned supreme, when many of the corpses were reft from seclusion to be boiled in a treacle tin stood on two bricks with stolen candle ends underneath. I can smell them now.[19]

Lilias as a young girl in a formal studio portrait. Cheyne Collection.

On her first holiday, a trip to Weymouth with her mother, Lilias wrote to her father in her usual affectionate way "My darling daddy" and told him that on a walk she had "noticed three things in nature" — rooks building their nests, a hedge starting to come out and the elder in full leaf. They had been for a boat ride and she had collected shells on the beach. She also told her father that when she next goes to London she wants to visit four attractions: South Kensington Museum ("as many times as possible"), the Zoo, Madame Tussaud's and ducks nesting at Regent's Park. This was a child with not only a love of animals but with

---

[19]   LRH, *Norfolk Notebook* (London: Faber and Faber, 1946), 53.

a definite inclination towards natural history.

Lilias was learning to read the garden.

2

The Lie of the Land

Beyond the estate at Ditchingham lay the extensive farmlands of East Anglia, largely unchanged for generations. The Haggards had farmed West Bradenham from the early nineteenth century; they had close links with many landed Norfolk families and a long involvement with the county as magistrates and in the militia. Their attitude to the land was imbued with affirmation of class, responsibility, regional pride and a sense of dynasty. The Margitsons, a military family, were less flamboyant and altogether more modest but had similar values.

Domestic life at Ditchingham followed a well-ordered routine managed very thoroughly by Louie thus giving Rider the structure and security he needed to maintain a steady production of fiction and later to expand his activities into public life. Under the benevolent hospitality of Louie and Rider the house gradually became a "lost dogs' home" for all the young Haggard cousins of whom there were thirty all told. Some were at boarding school while their parents lived abroad in service of the Empire or in the *Corps Diplomatique*; some occasionally needed respite from difficult circumstances. There was no chance of Lilias growing up in isolation. Some of these cousins would have been older than Lilias but she also had contemporaries in Sybil and Andrew, Will's younger children; three of Jack's four children (Joan, Andrew and Audrey) were all close to her in age, as

Lilias, centre, with a group of her boy cousins in a side doorway at Ditchingham House where pictures were regularly taken. Tom Haggard is top right. Cheyne Collection

were Arthur's sons Geoffrey and Rider and his daughter Phyllis. The Haggards'
position as gentry in the county meant that as she grew up there were parties,
shoots, croquet, and outdoor paper chases to keep everyone amused. Rider made
sure all the women in his family could handle a twelve bore and a revolver — use
of the latter was perhaps a remnant of colonial life. Theatrical *tableaux vivants*
were another favourite entertainment.

The estate was also home to a whole community of servants and farm workers
who would have been part of Lilias' world picture even though they were her
social inferiors. Ditchingham was very close to the market town of Bungay and
a host of small industries — silk weaving, maltings and brickworks — were in the
area as well as all the shops and farms. Respectable society quickly shelved off
into the murky areas of dire poverty where families struggled for the most basic
commodities. These people would have been off limits for Lilias as a girl although
not always for the boys in the family. Lilias' cousin Andrew (Jack and Aggie's
youngest son) wrote down his remembrances of staying at Ditchingham as a boy:

> When I was about fifteen I used to climb out of my bedroom
> window down an old pear tree and meet Rolfe [the poacher] on
> the Bath Hills at Ditchingham for a couple of hours villainy. One
> night we had eight pheasants there, and another three from the
> elm trees in the Rectory garden. I was terrified when old John
> Scudamore the parson poked his head out of the window and
> told us not to make too much noise, it was disturbing his rest.[1]

Louie thought that sea air was very important for children especially in the
autumn and around 1897–8 Rider bought two old coastguard properties facing
east across the North Sea at Kessingland.[2] The two houses were joined together
with a long passage and collectively called The Grange. The house provided the
Elysian joys of the beach and swimming for all the young Haggard children. With
his usual energy for the improvement of property Rider set to work:

> Rider sloped the cliff, which was falling away, planted marram
> grass to pile up the sand against the erosion of the sea — dug
> a new well and put a windmill to pump; made a new vegetable
> garden and generally enjoyed himself with improvements
> and additions. This house had a curious and very pleasant
> atmosphere. The many-windowed rooms were filled with clear,
> shadowless light and the smell and the sound of the sea. Week
> in and week out the gales from the north and the east roared

1   *The Things in My House*, a memoir by Andrew Haggard. HAG 224, Norfolk
     Record Office, page 7.
2   From LRH *Too Late for Tears*.

Kessingland Grange. Cheyne Collection.

over its low roof, cutting every living thing to the ground with
their salt-laden breath, so that special shelter had to be provided
before anything would grow at all.[3]

He named the bedrooms after English admirals and the walls were hung with
what sounds like the over-spill of furnishings, pictures and memorabilia from
Ditchingham.

> To his children and their young cousins, who spent many happy
> weeks there every year, it was an enchanted ground. They knew
> the creak of every door, the tick of every clock, the smell of every
> room. The grey seas, the windswept, deserted cliffs, and the great
> stretch of wide beach, which in those days was untrodden by any
> summer visitors, were their playground.[4]

With or without company, a child has an inner life and it was at the free
atmosphere of Kessingland that Lilias began to let her imagination play. She
recounted that the house was hung with the original illustrations from her father's
books and while she was slow to read she made up her own stories to attach to
the vivid and often lurid pictures. She was a great daydreamer as she recounted
years later:

> I have a collection of samplers [practice pieces of embroidery
> stitches made by children], which used to hang upon the walls

3   LRH *The Cloak that I Left,* 193.
4   Ibid,193.

of a many-windowed sitting-room of the house we had upon
the edge of the cliff at Kessingland. Many an hour I spent as a
small child, sitting at the gate-legged table with my lesson books,
listening to the sound of the sea, and making up stories about
the children who worked them instead of attending to hated
arithmetic and grammar. I was hopelessly bad at lessons, except
for a few subjects which interested me; they were so difficult and
day-dreaming was so easy.[5]

While the physical circumstances of her upbringing were privileged there were
undercurrents and conflicts below the surface that deeply affected her emotional
development. Her father's creativity and imagination were remarkable,
outstanding, but he had lost emotional intimacy with Lilias' mother, Louie,
and she with him. There was great respect and social compatibility; he wrote
to her every day when they were apart but there was no passion between them.
They lived their own lives in the same household. Louie was a strong woman,
physically and morally, not liberated in the modern sense, but more than able to
hold her own. Rider recounted in a letter that on one occasion after dinner she
had stayed up until midnight arguing with one of their guests on a political point.
All of the Ditchingham estate and the many houses that came with it had been
her inheritance before she married Rider but her nephew, Godfrey, in a letter of
1912, said that Louie was not a supporter of women's suffrage believing that "the
hand that rocked the cradle ruled the world".

Rider recounted that when they first returned to London from Africa they had
both seen a beautiful woman in the church congregation and both determined
to write a story about her; Louie had given up the attempt but Rider pursued the
work and wrote *Dawn* which was his first published novel. There are no further
accounts of him discussing his work with his wife; he soon found another help-
mate for developing his craft in Agnes Barber, an old school friend of Louie's, who
lived with them for several years to help with the children and then married his
brother Jack. Agnes, known as Aggie, had a psychic sensibility which fascinated
him and she wrote several interesting and competent novels of colonial life
herself.

When it came to passion Rider had never been able to relinquish his youthful
love for Lilly Jackson, an heiress slightly older than himself whom he had met just
before he left for Africa as a young man of nineteen. Her looks were sultry, dark
and heavy but the only indications of her character are circumstantial. In his
over-bearing, meddling way William Haggard forbade the match — on what basis
is not quite clear except that Rider was very young and his father wanted him to

5   LRH, *A Country Scrapbook* (London: Faber, 1950), 66.

establish his career; Lilly, with her substantial inheritance, would have been a good catch. Thwarted, Rider's sexual love for her became a consuming and life-long passion. While he was still in Africa and still hoping to win her hand, Lilly married Francis Archer, the guardian of her fortune.

The story of their marriage was not pretty. Archer was unscrupulous; he spent her money with ease, fled from his debts to Africa, insisted on her joining him and by 1904 had given her syphilis. Lilly's brother, Frederick Jackson, who made his life as a naturalist and hunter in Kenya had been at Cambridge with Arthur Haggard and entered the family circle becoming great friends with Rider and Louie. Nor did Lilly herself disappear; at various times she was living near Rider, first in London, then Criccieth, Wales, where they holidayed, and later in Norfolk. She was rarely far away. After Archer's death in Africa Rider took financial responsibility for at least two of her sons and, when she was living at the Red House in Aldeburgh with her sisters, helped her through the final stage of her dreadful illness. Both Rider and Louie visited her there and attended her funeral in Aldeburgh church in April 1909, as Rider's biographer D.S. Higgins discovered.

A great deal was going on in the Haggard family that was never talked about but Rider filled his novels with echoes of his yearnings, of unhappy marriages and rivalries for love and, most notably in *She*, of his desire for consummation of his passion in another, immortal, world. He treats the same theme in a variety of ways, for example as "three destinies" in *Stella Fregelius*.[6] In this story he harnessed his knowledge of the Danish legends with the stormy Suffolk coast north of Aldeburgh where the ruins of Dunwich lie beneath the waves. The hero's desires are divided between his fiancée, Mary, an earthly, practical woman and a spiritual, mystical woman, Stella, whom he saves from shipwreck. When Stella dies Rider's hero, "a mystic and a dreamer; one who dwells in the past and — in the future" is consumed by his passion for her for, as he explained "there is no human passion like this passion for the dead; none so awful, none so holy, none so changeless".[7]

All families have secrets, but this was heady stuff. The fact that Rider and Louie maintained a stable, vivacious and usually kindly household can be attributed to Louie's good sense[8] and to Rider's wry humour and increasingly humanitarian

---

[6]   It was written during 1902–3 and published by Longmans in 1904. D.S. Higgins thought that Rider may have taken the manuscript with him to Florence for Aggie's comments since he dedicated it to her by way of her nom-de-plume "John Berwick"; see *Rider Haggard the Great Storyteller*, 183.

[7]   LRH *Stella Fregellius*, (London: Hodder and Stoughton, 1923), 249 .

[8]   The household is likely to have been run on quite rigid lines. When Lilias was grown up and staying in their London flat she was expected to make a list of all the linen. She also had to present accounts for the spending of her allowance when she was well into her twenties.

views which, however, did not extend to any fundamental critique of colonialism or of the actual social structure in England. That critique was not outside Rider's awareness; his older brother Alfred had resigned from the Indian Civil Service on the grounds of the intrinsic injustice of imperialism, although he too had subsequently tried unsuccessfully to make his fortune in Africa. But Rider's dominant loyalty was always to his family; it fell to him to help raise the children of his more impecunious brothers which he did without complaint.

Rider had become frustrated by the limitations of writing endless romances, and when Lilias was about seven years old he began to develop a new political crusade around the future of agriculture at home and in the colonies. He wrote *A Farmer's Year* in serial form for *Longman's Magazine* and it was published as a whole in 1899. This diary format which combined a steady observation of the state of his farmland and the state of agriculture in England was very successful. Rider made a plea for better working conditions and old age pensions for agricultural labourers for whom he had great respect; he knew well the working classes' horror of the workhouse and shared hat view. Occasionally his entertaining prose opens to the terrifying reality of human life and he seems to surprise even himself as when he visited Heckingham workhouse, a few miles north west of Ditchingham:

> What do these old fellows think about, I wonder, as they hobble to and fro round those measureless precincts of bald brick? The sweet-eyed children that they begot and bred up to fifty years ago, perhaps, whose pet names they still remember, dead or lost to them for the most part; or the bright waving cornfields whence they scared birds when they were lads from whom death and trouble were yet a long way off. I dare say, too, that deeper problems worry them at times in some dim half-apprehended fashion; at least I thought so when the other day I sat behind two of them in a church near the workhouse. They could not read, and I doubt if they understood much of what was passing, but I observed consideration in their eyes. Of what? Of the terror and the marvel of existence, perhaps, and of that good god whereof the parson is talking in those long unmeaning words. God! They know more of the devil and all his works; ill-paid labour, poverty, pain, and infinite unrecorded tragedies of humble lives. God! They have never found Him. He must live beyond the workhouse wall — out there in the graveyard — in the waterlogged holes which very shortly ... [9]

---

[9]   H. Rider Haggard, *A Farmer's Year* (London: Cresset library edition, 1987), 430–431.

He had been engaged by the *Daily Express* to write about South Africa but with the outbreak of the second Boer War the editor had second thoughts. So Rider proposed an agricultural survey of all the counties in England — inspired by the agricultural pioneer, Arthur Young (1741–1820). This was an ambitious project but fortunately he was able to entice his old friend Arthur Cochrane — living in Kent and married with three children — to help him. Arthur accompanied him and filled up the notebooks which are now in the Norfolk Record Office. *Rural England* was published in 1902 and is still a source book for rural history. Inevitably Rider was spending long periods of time away from home but he needed both the income and the mental stimulation. During the winter of 1900–1901 the whole family decamped to Florence to stay with Uncle Jack and Aunt Aggie but they were plagued with influenza. Rider travelled on to Cyprus and the Holy Land searching for new material for both fiction and non-fiction. He was accompanied only by his nephew, Arthur Green (Ella's and Charles' son), acting as his secretary — an arrangement that turned out to be less than satisfactory from Rider's point of view since Arthur was not very competent.   Nevertheless, Rider was able to produce *A Winter Pilgrimage* and *The Brethren*, both published in 1904. In 1903 he gave up the lease of his farm in

Arthur Cochrane as a young man.
Courtesy of Una Cochrane.

Bedingham; his income had dropped by a third but he managed a second visit to Egypt in 1904 taking his eldest daughter Angela with him.

Angie and Dolly were growing up. Young upper class girls moved directly from childhood into adulthood and were launched socially into the adult world as a precursor to marriage. The moment of this change was called "coming out" when they were presented at Court to the King and Queen, an occasion that was followed by a round of well-chaperoned social events during which it was intended that they would find husbands. Angie and Dolly came out together in 1905 or 1906.

Lilias was still in the schoolroom and a governess joined the household, a Miss Hastings, of whom no trace is left. Lilias' interests remained almost entirely with animals and birds.

> When I reached my teens I was given a dog of my own, some racing pigeons, and allowed to keep hens, ducks and guinea fowls. Odd moments were filled up with trying to rear every sort of motherless young bird and animal, including (quite successfully) a litter of young hedgehogs with a fountain pen filler. The homing pigeons gave me hours of delight, as my father had a loft made for me, and the family good-naturedly carted baskets of young pigeons when they went on long trips in the car and let them off, while I sat at home waiting to clock them in.[10]

She not only reared them and studied their habits but developed an instinctive communication with some of them.

Meanwhile, Rider had had a dream that presaged the death of a much loved dog and vowed never to knowingly kill another living thing. He had become convinced that animals had souls. Ayesha, the heroine of *She*, continued to haunt him and in 1904 while he was at home he wrote *Ayesha: The Return of She* which was first published in serial form with dramatic illustrations by Maurice Grieffenhagen.[11]

In this and in later works, Rider reintroduced the mythology of Isis and Osiris which had been erased during the Christian era; he was bringing back the lost symbolism of the ancient goddess to Western culture. His preoccupation with the mythology of Ayesha reflected his attempts to resolve his own problems with his feminine side — what Jung called the *anima*.[12]

At around this time, possibly 1906, Lilias suffered from rheumatic fever that results from streptococcal

Angie, Dolly and their mother in trained dresses for their 'coming out' at Court.
Cheyne Collection.

10   LRH, *A Country Scrapbook* newspaper column, undated, post WWII.
11   Maurice Greiffenhagen (1862–1931) was a Royal Acadamician and a friend of Rider's.
12   For detailed discussion of this issue see Cornelia Brunner, *Anima As Fate* (Dallas: Spring publications, 1986), 113–15.

infection which is now uncommon in developed countries but used to be a major cause of childhood fatality. It can cause disease in the cardiac valves, and in Lilias' case almost certainly did. All illnesses were alarming in the Haggard household because of Rider's intense nervous anxiety that another loved one might be lost; Louie and all three daughters tried to hide any health problems.

In September of 1907 Angie married her cousin Tom Haggard after a discreet courtship since his mother, Judy, had been estranged from Rider and Louie for some years.[13] However, after initial concern about marriage between first cousins, Rider and Louie welcomed the match which they hoped would smooth over the former rift and there was always the possibility of a new "Haggard" heir.

From May of 1908, Lilias was sent to board at St Felix School near Southwold. It was just at this time that Rider and Louie were visiting the dying Lilly Jackson further down the East Anglian coast at Aldeburgh.

Rider's letter to her of June 2 1908 indicates that school life was a shock to her system:

> My dearest Lilias,
>
> You don't say when your half term is. If we are at Ditchingham of course we will arrange for you to come over.
> All "rules" are a bore, my dear, but in life we have to "play the game" and in one way or another are always running up against "rules". School rules, after all are but passing things, and not so very irksome when one gets used to them. But they are good training and discipline, as you will acknowledge afterwards. Meanwhile the thing is to fall in with them, however annoying, and wait. So, so long as you are well and happy in other respects, I should not bother about such trifles.
> Godfrey[14] has got a splendid appointment (as the result of passing his examination!). He is going out to Guatemala, practically to act as British Minister there. I am awfully glad about it. You should write to congratulate him. Ditchingham House will be his best address letters will always be forwarded.
> With best love your loving father
> H Rider Haggard[15]

---

13   Her cousin Harry Haggard in a letter to his mother, Alice, in November 1910 said Tom was "fat and floppy" and that "Angie is too good for him". Letter in the Lister collection.

14   Godfrey Haggard, son of Alfred and Alice, had a distinguished diplomatic career and left an unpublished memoir.

15   Cheyne Collection.

Wedding photograph of Angie and Tom Haggard, Ditchingham, 1907. Lilias is a bridesmaid on the far left. Cheyne Collection.

St Felix was a relatively new establishment which had been founded initially in Aldeburgh in 1892 by a Miss Gardiner with an emphasis on sensible education without competition thus allowing girls to advance at their own pace. The few restrictions and rules were enforced in the houses by prefects. Nevertheless, cold baths and outdoor games several times a week were the order of the day and Lilias also took riding lessons. The boarding houses were named after women who had contributed to emancipation: Jemima Clough, Millicent Fawcett, Elizabeth Fry and Florence Nightingale.[16] Lilias was in Fawcett House.

It was a time of much change at the school. Miss Gardiner had been taken ill in 1907, perhaps from nervous exhaustion. While she planned to return nothing could be done to replace her and it was not until 1908 that she resigned. During the hiatus pupil numbers declined sharply. Lilias arrived when rumours about her successor were rife. At one point it seemed that Miss Bate, house mistress of Fawcett might be appointed. Then Lilias heard that Miss Gardiner was confined to an asylum. According to a history of the school Miss Gardiner used to come back to the school secretly and go round the buildings in the moonlight and leave before dawn.[17]

16   Jemima Clough educator and co-founder of Newnham College, Cambridge; Millicent Fawcett suffragist and co-founder of Newnham College, Cambridge; Elizabeth Fry, prison reformer and anti-slave campaigner; Florence Nightingale, nursing in the Crimean war and hospital reformer.
17   Bernard Keeling, *Saint Felix School Southwold and The Old Felicians* (Kent: Longmore Press, 2001), 17.

In the autumn of 1908 Miss Lucy Silcox from Dulwich High School took on the role of headmistress. Lilias liked Miss Silcox but could not help noticing certain tendencies without perhaps really knowing what she was seeing. (Lilias' letters are not always grammatical and they are quoted in this book without correction.)

> I'm sending a photo of Miss Silcox, it is rather a black [sic] but she is fearfully dark her skin's like copper and her hair coal black, you can see how she sort of all goes thin below. She and the new drill mistress are awful friends you see them singing and playing to one another on Sunday evening. Miss Steadman has a simply glorious voice tho' you would <u>never</u> know it was not a man singing really I often think she must be a man dressed up! [18]

After the school photo was taken in 1909 she wrote home:

> I am going to bring one home so you will see Miss Silcox and Miss Steadman in their full glory. Miss Silcox is awfully sweet but everyone who sees her say there is something funny, I am perfectly certain she is half a Brahmin, or something, her room is full of foreign things . . . Miss Steadman is simply ripping too I am sending you another photo of her. She is exactly like a man of course. The other day when she was riding she asked a small boy to open a gate and he said "Yes, Sir". She got fearfully red and threw him a penny. The other day I overheard her say "It makes me laugh to think about it if you knew me for what I am, and here I am in a <u>boarding</u> school" with great stress on the boarding. Of course everyone knows the attraction is Miss Silcox, they simply worship one another. There is rather an upset in the school as 7 mistresses are leaving and I believe five Dulwich (Miss S's old school) ones coming so that means we shall have 6 Dulwich mistresses.[14]

At some time later after a half term or a holiday it was announced that Miss Bate was leaving. Lilias wrote to her mother:

> I never thought about such a thing happening I can't make out why she should leave her house which she is awfully fond of except that she is very bitter about Miss Silcox and I don't think likes her very much . . . What is worse Miss Fleming who is like a sister almost and adores her is leaving too! [19]

In another letter she added:

> The seven new mistresses are rather nice but some decidedly

[18]   Cheyne Collection.
[19]   Cheyne Collection

queer, rather the same type as Miss Silcox and they wear huge
pink and green pinafores! It's rather funny they all look rather
like men, and their names end in "man" Miss Colman, Miss
Steadman, Miss Seaman, Miss Freeman. We are going to learn
chemistry this term instead of Botany which will be ripping and
all Greek His: instead of English which is not so nice as I like
English History awfully. [20]

Lilias' letters home to her parents give us the first sound of her voice as a young
adult. They also show that her spelling was very careless although it improved
slightly during her time at school. The writing style is immediate, casual, and full
of enthusiastic slang: "spiffing" and "ripping" abound. The letters are nearly all
undated but some can be anchored by events and seasons; she was only at the
school for eighteen months, leaving in December of 1909 after her 18th birthday.
Her letters reveal her to be boisterous, affectionate, confident and humorous.
Even though St Felix wasn't far away she hated being away from home. She lived
for the afternoons out and the weekend exeats; her greatest pleasure at school lay
in the infrequent occasions when she could roam the countryside on her own.

Lilias had known
nothing but a safe and
affluent home. She arrived
at school by chauffeur
driven car, asked for her
side saddle to be sent
on along with a number
of other things she had
forgotten, evidently had a
camera of her own — and
was wilful and forthright
about arrangements.
Noticeably all the letters
are very affectionate
towards her parents, very
frank and open but the
range of discussion is very
limited; her horizons have
already been determined.
She did not mind
recounting pranks and was

Lilias as a teenager.

[20]   Ibid,

quick to admit to any misdemeanours — she trusted her parents to understand her and that she would never do anything underhand or deceitful.

> Miss Daniel [new head of Fawcett House] is really quite nice she did not even scold when she caught me last night pulling Olive Pulley downstairs by her leg. I tremble to think what Miss Bate would have said, the roof would have flown off. Could you please ask Mary[,]Mum [,] to send my dark blue Cathedral Psalter in my room or in the small cupboard, my long dancing gloves, and dancing shoes if she <u>can</u> find them as they are not here and I must have them . . . [21]

Lilias seems to have nearly as much trouble as her father with leaving things behind ". . . I discovered I had left my handbag in the motor!!!! Imagine my horror as it contained my watch keys fountain pen, £1 and health certificate . . ."[22] We would consider her quite young for her age - at seventeen she was still having pillow fights — but she was aware that some of her contemporaries had been thrust into adult concerns already. She had heard of a girl who, at the age of sixteen, was married and had a baby and was keenly aware of one girl at school who had lost both parents and several siblings to fatal illnesses.

For Lilias there was no real rebellion and perhaps no crises of development such as became common for younger people in the later part of the twentieth century. While she was pleasantly self-deprecating she did not engage in self-reflection. If the surface was still that did not mean there was no activity in her depths. Many years later in a newspaper article she recalled the lasting impression that her headmistress had made upon her and a terrifying dream in which the headmistress was making a speech about the wisdom and influence of women. In the dream Lilias was to present her with a green basalt head of an Egyptian queen but when she suddenly unwrapped the package Lilias was horrified to see not the lovely queen's head but her father's inkpot made from the hoof of his favourite horse, Moresco. Lilias woke up in a complete panic.[23] Here is some insight into Lilias' subconscious knowledge that her "gift" or talent is from her father but perhaps from a base level — the horse's hoof, and also that she is missing the "queen" — the higher female self.

At a mundane level Lilias accepted the social pattern of behaviour expected of her. Confident herself, she was not above teasing other girls who were less so, and was surprised when she met with an unhappy response. When her housemistress called her behaviour "boisterous" she wrote home, "Fancy calling <u>that</u> being

21   Ibid, letter 36.
22   Ibid, letter 2.
23   Article for the *EDP*, May 21st 1955, "What should Miss H. Do."

boisterous, Oh I <u>should</u> like to take her home collect every cousin we posses and let her hear what <u>real</u> noise was."[24] Brought up as she was in the forthright atmosphere of the Haggards, she had already developed a loud voice according to her housemistress and was not afraid to use it to announce her views.

A school friend, writing to the family after Lilias' death, said, "I know Lilias hated games and the gym and its contents, especially the vaulting horse, were her nightmare. All her talent was literary. She once told me and my sister we had no ambition! True I am afraid."[25]

Lilias began to try her hand at writing articles; the first was a fairy story about Isis for a magazine after which Miss Daniel asked her to write an article for the *Felician* school magazine. Her father's occasional comments on her writing were affirming and encouraging: "No dear your letters don't bore me at all. They are very good letters: you should always write like that — naturally."[26] When she was asked to take part in a debate she wrote home to her father at once asking for points to make. She was aligning herself with him almost as an aspiring colleague; psychologically she was identifying with him. She noted subjects that might interest him such as a lecture she heard about the de la Pole family of Suffolk which stayed in her mind fermenting until much later.

Apart from her interest in history and writing, the one subject she excelled in was chemistry. If she had had a good basic education, especially in maths, she might have developed a scientific career since her interest in nature was so pronounced. Rider gave some passing acknowledgement to this possibility. While he was staying at Carrow Abbey, the Norwich home of the Colman family, and meeting the Chancellor of the Exchequer Mr Lloyd George, he took the time to write to her:

> Do they teach you any chemistry? I believe there is a good
> opening for women in practical chemistry if they happen to have
> a taste for it and can follow it up.[27]

When Sir William ffolkes of Hillington Hall, Norfolk, a friend of Rider's, gave a talk to the girls at St Felix. Rider suggested that Lilias write to him. Rider was initiating her into adult ways of cultivating connections, a social skill to which Rider (and his father before him) always paid attention. She was recognised as something of a tomboy and her father often included in his letters to her details about machinery or livestock, an interest that they shared. By now Lilias was a good-looking girl, not especially tall but with an open bright face. It must have helped her at school to have such a famous father and she seems to have been popular:

24   Cheyne Collection .
25   Olive Robins (her married name) writing from Ashford, Kent to Mark Cheyne on August 1st 1970. Letter in Cheyne Collection.
26   Letter from HRH to LRH, June 2nd 1908, Cheyne Collection.
27   HRH to LRH July 5th 1908, Cheyne Collection.

Do you think it would be possible Mummy for me to bring three
or four girls over to have tea one afternoon I should like to as
they ask me out.[28]

Her old school friend, Olive Robbins, writing in 1970, recalled, "On one
occasion she took me with another girl to their lovely place perched high on
the cliff at Kessingland, I think. I was greatly awed by her parents but it was a
memorable day."[29] Rider did his part as a parent and made a contribution to the
fund-raising for a new school hall at St Felix.

Dolly, Lilias' eldest sister, had become engaged to a Major Reginald Cheyne
(1870–1955) of the Indian Army whom she had met while staying with her aunt
and uncle, Baron and Baroness d'Anethan, in Japan. This caused considerable
excitement and the Major was brought down to St Felix to meet Lilias. After many
letters and arrangements Lilias managed to get three days off for the wedding in
July 1908 at which she was a bridesmaid.

In 1911 a two-reel film version of *She* was released in the USA by the
Thannhauser Production Company. A short scene of *Ayesha La Danse de Feu* had
been made in France as early as 1899, and in 1908 an Edison Production company
had produced a very short version. Rider Haggard's name was known worldwide
giving Lilias quite a glamorous background but not one that was indulged by
Rider or Louie; at home his novel writing was rarely mentioned. Conversation
was on local matters and public affairs.

It was while Lilias was growing up that Rider shifted the emphasis of his career
from that of a romance writer to a public servant. Politically he belonged to the
Liberal Unionist Party – a group of Liberals who opposed Home Rule for Ireland
and attached themselves to the Conservative Party from 1886 to 1912 after which
they were absorbed into it. Rider was temperamentally a cross-bencher – a man
who would vote according to his conscience not his party – and could not hope to
find a serious home in party politics, but he was a good analyst, very popular in the
press and his voice was listened to. Governments could not afford to ignore him.

Rider's first commission had been in 1905 when the Rhodes Trust financed
an inquiry into the Salvation Army labour colonies in the United States. On this
trip, on which he was accompanied by his daughter Angie, he met and made
friends with Theodore Roosevelt – a man after his own heart. He also began
to advocate widespread settlement of the "empty" colonial lands in Canada and
Australia. From his official report he extracted a highlighted version for public
consumption called *The Poor and the Land*.

Haggard's first biographer, Morton Cohen, drew the conclusion that Rider

[28]   Cheyne Collection.
[29]   Letter from Olive Robbins in the Cheyne Collection.

Wedding photograph of Dolly and Reginald Cheyne, July 1908. Lilias is the bridesmaid immediately to the right of Dolly. Cheyne Collection.

realised that the land would not support three layers of the rural population — the owner, the farmer and the labourer — and it was the landowner who was superfluous.[30] He proposed socialist strategies to the ownership of land and in so doing, Cohen argued, Rider renounced his class heritage and, in this area at least, his Unionist Tory political loyalties. This analysis seems too clear cut. Although Rider was supportive of Lloyd George, the Liberal reformer, in his later *War Diaries* he railed loudly against socialists and communists and when unemployment insurance was introduced he complained about how hard it was get servants.

The 1906 election swept the Liberals into power and when Rider heard there was to be a Royal Commission on Coastal Erosion he proffered his knowledge of shoring up the cliffs at Kessingland with marram grass. He was duly appointed and began the committee and public work that was to dominate the rest of his life and take him all over the world. Biographer D.S. Higgins thought it was the government's way of diverting his energies away from what might have been awkward agricultural campaigns at home.[31] Haggard himself may have found it a way out of actively committing to his conclusions about landownership.

[30]   Morton Cohen, *Rider Haggard - His Life and Works* (London: Hutchinson, 19600.
[31]   D.S. Higgins, *Rider Haggard The Great Storyteller* (London: Cassell, 1981), 189.

Chapter 3
Rough Ground

Lilias left school in the December of 1909. Surviving letters written between Lilias and her parents are full of domestic anecdotes and relate the comings and goings of cousins, aunts, uncles and friends. They had busy lives and for Lilias much of it was social: tennis parties, picnics and dances. She also involved herself with animals and husbandry on the estate.

Despite the continuity of life in the country this was a time of great social change. Suffragettes continued to press vehemently for their cause. Long over-due attempts to meet the needs of urban industrial society were manifested in laws providing for Old Age Pensions and Labour Exchanges. In 1909 Lloyd George introduced his "People's Budget" which was thrown out by the House of Lords. After a General Election in 1910 returning Asquith as Prime Minister the upper house was forced to accept the taxation that would pay for social reforms and increased naval expenditure. The Lords were soon to lose their power to obstruct budgets. King Edward VII died in May 1910. Rider had finished his work on coastal erosion and was at a loose end and his income was declining despite frenetic bouts of romance writing.

When *The Times* commissioned a set of articles on the state of agriculture in Denmark, Rider seized the opportunity and set off

Lilias as a young woman. Cheyne Collection.

in September 1910 taking Lilias with him. He also invited Aggie, his sister-in-law and one-time muse, as his secretary; Aggie was by then a widow, Jack having died in 1908 in his last posting at Malaga, southern Spain. Between surveying Danish farms, they found time to visit Aagaard which the family believed to be their place of origin. [1]

Rural Denmark was published in its entirety by Longmans in the spring of 1911 and described the more egalitarian Danish style of farming. Afterwards, Rider, faced with inactivity and dull days at Ditchingham, sank into a depression during which he wrote his autobiography *The Days of My Life* that was to be published posthumously in two volumes. Lilias, although never presented at Court as her sisters had been,[2] was launched into adult social life. Aged nineteen, she travelled to Malta during 1911/12, undoubtedly staying with relatives or friends when she arrived. Her letters home to her father, which he kept, were destroyed in the 1940s. She attended the May Balls at Cambridge as the guest of the Longmans; Frederick Longman, the son of Charles Longman

A party of Longman family and friends May Week 1911. Lilias and Freddie Longman brimming over with fun, she standing second from left back row, he on one knee, far left front. Cheyne Collection.

[1]   Rider had previously visited Iceland, extensively researched the old Norse sagas, and written *Eric Brighteyes* published in 1891. Andrew Wawn in his book *The Vikings and the Victorians* (Cambridge: D.S. Brewer, 2000), 331, praises it as "arguably the finest Victorian Viking-age novel".

[2]   It was discussed in letters of 1912 between Lilias and her mother. Lilias was "not at all sorry" she wrote, "there is plenty of time for that". She later attended a garden party at Buckingham Palace.

who was one of Rider's publishers, was studying medicine at Pembroke. The photographs show Lilias dressed very smartly and elaborately in white with a huge hat and veil; she is smiling broadly and is full of vitality. After the balls Lilias went to stay with the Longmans who lived at Upp Hall, Braughing in Hertfordshire (where she signed the visitors' book) and it is possible that Frederick was a potential suitor. Rider recalled later that Frederick stayed with them at Ditchingham.

The following year Rider's luck changed: the new King George V conferred a knighthood on him and soon afterwards he was invited to be one of six British Royal Commissioners charged with undertaking a survey of the colonies over a three year period. Knowing that once the work began he would be fully occupied, Rider took his second daughter Angie on a trip to Egypt and southern Spain, and sailed early for India at the end of 1912 so he could visit Dolly and her husband, Major Cheyne, before joining the other commissioners in Australia. He didn't return home until June 1913.

Young Lilias at home with a pet rabbit.
Cheyne Collection.

In February 1912, while her mother was away on visits, Lilias stayed temporarily at Ditchingham Lodge with Muriel Turner, a cousin on her mother's side, who had three children including a little baby boy Eric who was apparently fragile. The Turners were leasing the Lodge. Later they moved to Tunney's Lane on the far side of Ditchingham. Lilias wrote to her mother about purchasing some birds — probably canaries — which she bred, about some redecorating, talking to Longrigg the farm manager, making social "calls" in the neighbourhood and about visiting her Cousin Rose Hildyard, now living in Hill House Road in Norwich.

Lilias had been suffering for some time from inexplicable tiredness and pain. In June 1912 Angie took her to see a Dr Williams and reported to her mother that Lilias' condition was not hysteria (as had presumably been suggested) but very real and that she needed an internal examination. In October of 1912 her brother-in-law, Tom, diagnosed her with a prolapsed left ovary and Lilias wrote to her mother regarding the necessary surgery: "I would rather have anything done almost than go through again what I have endured this last year." All details were carefully kept from Rider until afterwards.

Possibly as a recuperation holiday after the surgery, which was either removal of an ovary or a partial hysterectomy, Lilias made a visit to Brazil where her uncle Will was Envoy Extraordinary and Minister Plenipotentiary in Rio de Janeiro. In an undated letter from her Aunt Nitie to Louie there is discussion about a chaperone for the voyage out and also mention of the publication of a memoir by Baroness d'Anethan (Aunt Eleanora) called *Fourteen Years of Diplomatic life in Japan* which anchors the date around late 1912. The following year Lilias' sister Angie had a fallopian pregnancy (her second); she was given a full hysterectomy which finished any hope of children.

The second stage of Rider's commission work was to be in South Africa and he decided to take Louie and Lilias with him stopping at Madeira on the way. So it was that Lilias experienced first hand the places and people that had made such an impact on young Rider and then on both her parents in the early days of their marriage. She was immersed in events and relationships that had happened long before her birth: both reliving her father's story and watching him recall it in a mood of nostalgia. It was this experience that she was able to draw on many years later when she wrote her father's biography.

The third part of Rider's study took him to Canada in July 1914 but it was cut short by the events in Europe. At the outbreak of war with Germany he immediately began a War diary:

> St John's Newfoundland. 29th July 1914
> The Governor told me that he had received very serious advices
> from England, one of which was to the effect — "Watch cables
> and shipping. Make ready." Poor England — without an adequate
> army![3] I am very anxious, and wonder whether Armageddon has
> come at last.[4]

Lilias wrote to her father from Ditchingham on 13th August, just nine days after Britain declared war on Germany, about the mood and events unfolding:

> There is no more news lately and everything goes on as usual
> but of course we are all waiting for a big naval engagement on

---

[3]   Rider blamed Lord Haldane, the War Minister, for his reduction of troops by 30,000.

[4]   *The War Diaries of H. Rider Haggard*, typed transcript, Volume I, page 8.

the North Sea. Heaven knows what will happen when it comes, whoever wins the loss of life must be something enormous.

A lot of our troops have gone to Belgium although you won't find that in the papers. . . . I think some of our aeroplanes have gone as Captain Wallace and Mr Turner who were coming down next week for the tennis wrote that they would be the first to be sent! And they are attached to the squadron at Farnborough. The worst of it is so little news is allowed through, that one never knows what is going on.[5]

She went on to recount that horses were being bought up for the army at very good prices and one of her cousins, Audrey, who had been visiting Germany, was having trouble getting home. Lilias finished the letter with:

PS I should think you had much better stay in Canada there is nothing to do here except sit and wait.[6]

In the event all the members of the commission were recalled home and sailed from Quebec on August the 19th. With fuel shortages imminent Rider and Louie shut up the house and moved into a flat in London but with Rider's weak chest the winter fogs played havoc with his health. Rider at first found no role other than making energetic speeches urging young men to join up.

Lilias was now twenty-one, nearly twenty-two years old, and would normally have expected to marry within the next few years. Several of her cousins, the boys she had grown up with at Ditchingham, were already in the armed services when World War I started. Supporting the War was an unquestioned duty in the Haggard family. Her cousin Mark (Bazett's youngest son) in the Welch regiment died in one of the first September onslaughts, the battle of the Aisne, in a charge against German Maxim guns. Rider made every effort to find witnesses and record the exact details of his death. Mark had been shot in the stomach and although he was brought back behind the lines he probably never reached a hospital, dying some hours later in the trenches and buried in France. On November 12th Rider recorded the death of Freddie Longman who had joined the Royal Fusiliers, been wounded almost immediately, recovered in a hospital in France, and returned to the fray. Rider recorded "I fear his family will be desolated, for he was their idol" and when he met Longman in London he wrote, "I did not like to pursue the subject seeing that he looked distressed beyond bearing."[7] What Lilias may have

5   Cheyne Collection.
6   Ibid.
7   *The War Diaries of H. Rider Haggard* November 12th 1914, typed transcript
       Volume I, page 176.

felt Rider did not mention.

The war was having an immediate effect on social behaviour at home. Suddenly a new stream of steady income in the form of soldiers' wages was filtering through, both directly and through their wives, to the general working-class populace. The results, which were eventually to fuel social change in terms of better nutrition and housing, had side effects that were not appreciated locally. Rider wrote in his diary October 14th 1914:

> The bulk of the population do not seem at all to understand
> the seriousness of the crisis in our national affairs. One of the
> effects of the war is that numbers of older women, being better
> off, are drinking a great deal, while the young ones rejoice whole-
> heartedly the presence of so many soldiers in their midst and
> are to be met with them in every lane. In Norwich they say the
> thing has become such a scandal that no woman under twenty is
> allowed in the streets after ten pm.[8]

Lilias was home in Ditchingham during the autumn of 1914 while rumours and anxieties increased. Rider recorded on October 27th:

> Lilias has been to see Mrs Smith,[9] wife of Colonel Lockhart
> Smith, DSO, who is at present commanding a regiment of
> Kitchener's new army. Mrs Smith told her that there is a good
> deal in the rumours of some wireless installation that for some
> time past has been said to be working from the immediate
> neighbourhood, giving information, etc, to the Germans. It was
> first reported by our cruisers off the coast, which caught the
> messages.[10]

Reggie Cheyne had been transferred to General Pirie's staff and was being sent from India to the Front which meant that Dolly and her two boys were coming home.[11] Husband and wife travelled back on separate ships on a voyage that took five weeks. Dolly's nurse had been pre-paid which turned out to be a mistake since once they had embarked she flatly refused to do anything. Dolly was left to manage as best she could with two small children[12] on an over-crowded ship in extreme temperatures and no refrigeration for the food. The Captain was all for abandoning the rebellious nurse in Egypt and letting her fend for herself but

8   Ibid, October 14th 1914, typed transcript Volume 1, page 87.
9   The Smiths were living at Ellingham Hall.
10   *The War Diaries of H. Rider Haggard*, October 27th 1914, typed transcript Volume
      1, page 127/8.
11   Probably Major General Charles Pirie of the Ambala Cavalry Brigade, 15th
      Lancers Cureton Multanis, a Pathan regiment.
12   Their third child, Mark, was born in Budleigh Salterton, Devon in March 1917.

Dolly was too "kind-hearted" to allow it. At Port Said Reggie left the convoy and headed for Marseilles having managed to say good-bye to his wife. She was due in on a boat train at Paddington on November 15th but the line was blocked by troop trains heading for France which delayed her arrival by two hours. Louie, Angie and Tom waited for her but Rider had to leave them in the waiting room, fearing for his health in the cold and damp.[13] Not surprisingly soon after their arrival one of Dolly's sons was taken ill but fortunately recovered.

During this time Lilias was staying at Bradenham with her cousins where Will had retired from diplomatic service. Lilias was almost as familiar with the West Bradenham estate as she was with Ditchingham. The village church was filled with Haggard memorials and she would also have known the estate workers, the villagers and many of the stories and memories that were handed down from her uncles and aunts.

Towards the end of November the family heard that George Haggard, (eldest son of Bazett and Julia), who had been captured in France, had escaped from Brussels by bribing his sentry and obtaining a forged passport. In a rare lighter story of the war it transpired that the sentry had previously been employed as a waiter at the Carlton restaurant in London and remembered George from better days. In December Louie and Lilias went down to Dover to visit Hal, "They found him rather depressed. It appears that our fleet in the Channel dares not go out for fear of the German submarines."[14]

The next piece of news was that Archie Cheyne, Reggie's elder brother, had been wounded and was being nursed at 10 Carlton House Terrace. Rider went to visit him and noted that the house was like a palace and had a great marble staircase. Grand houses all over the country were being offered or requisitioned as hospitals and nursing homes; some of the regular soldiers must have been quite surprised at their surroundings. Rider and Louie seem to have spent the winter between London and St Leonard's on the south coast because of Rider's susceptibility to bronchitis. Lilias was at least some of the time in Ditchingham where she could hear the Zeppelins bombing Yarmouth. Rider had a letter from his nephew Lance (younger son of Arthur) who had volunteered with a Canadian regiment, Princess Patricia's Canadian Light Infantry; he recounted just how appalling the conditions were at the Front and that the cobbled roads in Flanders were a dreadfully painful surface to march along. It is likely that Lilias was helping Dolly with her children because Rider notes that they had been in Brighton in March. In April they were all back in Ditchingham and Rider went to visit some of the wounded soldiers being nursed at Hedenham Hall, a house owned by the

13   *The War Diaries of H. Rider Haggard,* typed transcript, November 15th and
      November 17th 1914, Volume 1, pages 185 and 186.
14   Ibid, December 14th 1914, Volume 1, page 232, typed transcript.

Carrs of Ditchingham Hall, in the next village to the north. Lilias' cousin Phoebe (eldest daughter of Jack and Aggie) married their cousin Dan (youngest son of Alfred and Alice) at Ditchingham and the wedding photo shows the groom in military uniform.

By the summer one of Lilias' cousins, Noel Hildyard, was nursing at a hospital in the north of England. Dolly had been able to go to Paris to spend time with her husband on leave. Lilias was undecided about what to do. She had already made some attempt at nursing training but was uncommitted and indeed rather nonchalant about the prospects. In a rather incoherent letter to her father she wrote about the possibility of taking a car — or perhaps an ambulance — out to the Front and whether to continue with her six-week VAD nursing course:

> Thanks ever so for your letter, the motor business is all very vague — personally I don't think either of us have the slightest chance of getting to France — Angie because she has a husband [Tom] there and me because of lack of experience. I only meant to chuck nursing for the summer because it's rather a pull in the hot weather and also because I don't want Angie to go alone as I am sure she would hate it. It takes us six weeks to get through the course and we can't do anything till then and I shan't arrange anything without asking you both, I am not going canteening [working in the canteens] even if she does as I don't see the fun of paying all one's expenses — it's not worth it. Meanwhile it's an awfully useful thing to have one's certificate so if she really does go for this course I should like to too.[15]

Lilias before the war, from her own photograph album.
Cheyne Collection.

According to Rider's diary, in August 1915 Lilias was at "Dalling" [probably Wood Dalling in Norfolk] either doing war work, or perhaps training. In September she accompanied her father on a fortnight's fishing holiday to Galway in Ireland. There were rumours of the Commission starting up again but nothing confirmed and Rider waited for some useful role. Then in October 1915 Rider wrote that "John Kipling, Rudyard Kipling's son, whom I have known from a child, is wounded and missing, but there is still hope that he may be a prisoner as he was not severely hurt when last seen." On October 18th he wrote about the execution of Edith Cavell, "She fainted . . . in the presence of the firing party, whereupon the officer in charge blew her brains out with a revolver."[16] It was becoming clear that the war wasn't going to end any time soon and also that German behaviour both on and off the battlefield was galvanising people's position on the war.

Wedding photograph of Dan and Phoebe Haggard. Cheyne Collection.

The Voluntary Aid Detachment (VAD) had been founded by the War Office in the wake of the Boer War, part of the same initiative that set up the Territorial Army, and provided field nursing services mainly in hospitals; about two thirds of the volunteers were female and came from the middle and upper middle classes. There were already 2,500 Voluntary Aid Detachments in 1914 and VAD hospitals were soon opened in most large towns in Britain. These had to be financed by the County Finance Committees and by massive and continual fund-raising. The organisation and discipline was military with a Medical Officer in charge of each hospital and a chain of authority through Matrons and Sisters.

There were two kinds of VAD helpers — General Service and VAD nursing aides who received basic first aid and home nursing training. At first their minimal skills led to friction with trained nursing professionals and there was often an unbridgeable class difference as well. Daily life without servants was a severe shock to upper class girls, who were often doing the work of cleaners, and

---

[16]   This was a rumour. Subsequent investigations have shown that she was shot by the firing squad.

so also was the discipline of hospital work; how they adapted to the conditions depended on their individual characters and whether they were able to learn from their working experience. For those who did adapt there was another hurdle of discouragement from the fact that there was no career path or seniority — once a VAD always a VAD. Their dedication had to come solely from a sense of duty, patriotism and compassion.

The VADs wore a regulation uniform of mid-blue overalls, white over-sleeves and a large white apron with a red cross on the bodice — although a shortage of red fabric later in the war led to plain aprons. They had stiff white collars and cuffs and a starched white cap, replaced in due course by a more distinctive large white handkerchief or scarf tied at the nape of the neck. They were not at first sent to the front as nurses but did go as canteen workers and cooks and to replace the male orderlies. Before long the sheer numbers of casualties broke down this restriction and there were many VADs at hospitals in France. Outside Britain, the initial generous allowances that even the least experienced received led to resentments from the professional nurses and in 1916 allowances were converted to an annual £20 payment, £4 for their uniform plus all living expenses. Those who came from well-to-do families were expected to pay for themselves. VADs in Britain were unpaid until rising prices made it more and more difficult for most of them to survive on what their families could give them and they too became the recipients of small salaries.

During the war the VAD came under the jurisdiction of the Red Cross and the St John Ambulance Service and was centrally administered from Devonshire House, courtesy of the Duke and Duchess of Devonshire.

The VAD Commander-in-Chief was Katharine Furse (1875–1952).[17] It was this organisation that Lilias decided to join on November 23rd 1915 and which she served, according to her record, as a nursing assistant until February 28th 1918. According to her minimal Red Cross record Lilias' first posting, which lasted about fourteen months, was just up the road from Ditchingham at Hedenham Hall already mentioned, which was being used as a VAD hospital. During this period there are no surviving letters but there is an album of photographs that shows only too graphically that Lilias was working with amputees.

If the start of the war had been slightly unreal the effects were now on her doorstep. Kitty Carr, one of four siblings and just a few years younger than Lilias, met at a dance a young army officer who had been invalided home. According to their daughter Diana Athill, they kissed in the conservatory and that was enough in those days to trigger an engagement. They married the following year and it is

17   Furse, having pioneered the work of the Detachment, resigned in 1917 frustrated by the lack of power to reorganise and reform. She was immediately employed by the Women's Royal Naval Service who recognised her ability.

most likely that members of the Haggard family attended their wedding.[18]

By December 1915 still nothing had been heard of Jack Kipling and Rider interviewed a young wounded soldier named Bowe from the Irish Guards in an attempt to discover what had happened but his account was inconclusive. Then at the end of December, Lilias received a letter from another soldier, Frankland, who was better educated and sent fresh details gleaned from Bowe. He had witnessed Jack Kipling with a dreadful mouth wound from shrapnel. His disappearance was still a mystery.

In February 1916 Rider set off again to visit the colonies, this time as an honorary representative of the Royal Colonial Institute to inquire into after-the-war settlement of sailors and soldiers. It was not a government role and while Rider had a popular following, Canadian immigration officials found his interference impertinent, especially when they realised that the RCI was raising money from Canadian businessmen to pay his fares.[19]

Lilias, Louie and Angie saw him off at Paddington, heading first for Cape Town via Madeira on the Kenilworth Castle. He arrived in South Africa on February 28th. The Governor, Lord Buxton, was too anxious about upsetting the Nationalist Party to offer land in South Africa itself but the chartered board of the British South Africa Company offered half a million acres of land in Rhodesia for soldier settlers and free passage for families and sweethearts. Rider also had discussions with the Prime Minister, General Botha, about establishing a "Cape Route to Australasia" to tie the Empire together. Political sensitivities forced Rider to avoid much public speaking. He left in mid-March and arrived in Hobart, Tasmania early in April and was glad to have the promise of land for three hundred men. His tour of Australia was long and tiring and fraught with political difficulties but he received a number of promises of support — including a million acres of dairy and agricultural land in Queensland. During this trip Rider heard from Louie of the death of his older brother Alfred.

In June he moved on to New Zealand where news reached him of the success of the film version by H. Lisle Lucoque of She starring Alice Delysia. While in Auckland on June 11th he attended a Memorial Service for Lord Kitchener, who had died when the HMS Hampshire hit a mine off Orkney. Rider wrote: "For my part I could not help thinking of the six or seven hundreds of good men and true who went to doom with him. But of these we heard little of nothing. Such is the world."

He took most pleasure in the singing of the South Sea Farewell by a native woman in Honolulu. He reached Victoria, British Columbia on the 29th June to

18   Diana Athill_Life Class, (London: Granta, 2002) 100. Typical of her class and generation Kitty knew nothing about sex or of her own preferences with regard to men.
19   Victoria Manthorpe, Children of the Empire (London: Gollancz, 1986), 219.

Photographs from Hedenham Hall VAD hospital from Lilias' photograph album. Cheyne Collection

be met by his younger brother Andrew who had settled there with his third wife, Ethel. After a short stay at Andrew's house near Cowichan Lake, Rider moved to the Empress Hotel and began his work again. He travelled by train across Canada stopping in each province to ask for promises of farm land for settlers. The trans-continental journey culminated in a meeting with President Roosevelt at his home Sagamore Hill on Oyster Bay, New York State. The two men talked freely and amicably about world affairs and about when America would come into the war. Rider arrived home at the end of July 1916 utterly exhausted and his doctor ordered him not to travel again for some time. On August 3rd he recorded in his diary that Lilias, her cousin Joan and Dorothy Carr went to a dance in Bungay at the invitation of a Colonel after which there was Zeppelin raid and the whole household retreated to the cellar.

    While staying in London in September Rider, Louie, Angie and their old friend Mrs Jebb went to the cinema to see a film about the Somme. Even though the film seems to have highlighted the courage and bravery of the soldiers and not the full devastation of the trenches, Rider found it appalling.

In October Rider sat for his portrait to William Strang who afterwards also painted Lilias: the portrait is on the front cover of this book.[20] Rider thought he had made her "too serious and a little scornful which is not her character — although she is determined".

Rider and Louie spent the winter of 1916/17 at Budleigh Salterton in Devon where Alice, the recently widowed wife of Alfred, had family ties and it was close to where Lilias had been posted to the Exmouth VAD Hospital. Her Red Cross service card gives her arrival as January 1st 1917 but according to *Red Cross and Voluntary Aid in Devonshire 1914-17* Lilias may have arrived as early as November 1916 — towards the end of the Battle of the Somme. Her letters give the impression of often being called in at a moment's notice, possibly on an initially temporary basis, which may account for the discrepancy.

The Red Cross Committee in Devon was chaired by Countess Fortescue and comprised Lady Audrey Buller,[21] Lady Marion Stanley, Miss Boggis, Lord Fortescue KCB (who was also Lord Lieutenant of the county and an ADC to the King) and Lady Amory — all representatives of the gentry and ruling class. *Voluntary Aid in Devon 1915* edited by W. Fothergill Robinson explains that the Voluntary Aid Detachment obtained a temporary hospital in Exmouth by converting The Sailor's Rest on St Andrew's Road

> . . . block 1 contains one large ward and three small wards, also an excellent operating theatre which has been much admired, a recreation room for the men, and the Detachment office. Block 2 has one large ward, and the matron's quarters. A third block is contemplated in the YMCA building close by, which will provide enough beds to make a total of fifty. A lawn between the two buildings has served admirably for bowls etc, for the convalescents. After mobilisation, Block 1 was furnished and equipped with fifteen beds, and opened on October 11th 1914, while Block 2 with fourteen beds was opened November 28th. Most of the articles were requisitioned, and it is owing to the kindness of many friends that the cost of fitting up the hospital

[20]   He had also painted Kitty Carr.
[21]   *The Exeter Western Times* reported on April 9th 1914 that Lady Buller had accepted the Presidency of the Exeter branch of the National Society for Opposing Women's Suffrage because Lady Fortescue had found herself unable to attend to the duties owing to the long distance from Exeter to her residence, which was Castle Hill near Barnstable. Lady Fortescue had been born Emily Ormesby-Gore, a daughter of Lord Harlech.

(exclusive of the theatre) did not exceed £40. The Linen
League in Exeter and the Linen Depot in Exmouth both made
substantial grants.

The hospital was used to inoculate Territorial soldiers against enteric fever
and then to treat casualties from the Expeditionary Force. The editor notes that:

> "The wounded and sick men benefit greatly by the air of
> Exmouth, and the great kindness of many friends in lending
> them their motor cars has been a factor in their recovery, as it
> has enabled the frost-bitten and crippled to enjoy the bracing
> air of Woodbury Common, and revel in the beautiful scenery
> abounding in every direction.

Exeter VAD Hospital from Voluntary Aid in Devon 1915 *edited by W. Fothergill.*

> "The concerts given frequently by the fellow townspeople [sic]
> has been much appreciated by the patients and staff".

Red Cross and Voluntary Aid in Devonshire 1914-17 [22] gives the further information
that by 1917 there were seventy-three beds, that the Officer in Command was Dr J.
W. Hodgson and the Matron was Mrs Florence Tilbury. In a list of VAD nurses is
the name "Miss Rider Haggard Nov 1916 — February 1917. " "Early in 1917 Block I
was re-equipped to receive officers only, leaving Block II and III for other ranks."[23]

[22]   Exeter: M A Rudd and Son, 1917
[23]   *Red Cross and Voluntary Aid in Devonshire 1914-17*, 84.

Improvements included electrical and mechanical appliances including an X-ray machine and whirlpool baths for massage.

In an undated letter written soon after she arrived Lilias wrote to her mother:

> All serene so far but I think I have landed in a queer spot it's a
> most casual spot anyhow as far as I can make out and there's no
> order or method anywhere, the nurses do everything even the
> dressings of the serious cases, but I will tell you all about it if
> you are coming over tomorrow......the work here is not really
> hard but very tiring as it gets so muddled and no one knows
> what to do and when, one man in my block is dying fast which
> is a cheerful beginning for me, as poor boy he's in dreadful pain
> except when under Morphia. The Matron is away, she left this
> morning as her little boy is very ill with measles caught I believe
> when he was staying here.
>
> If you do come over tomorrow come to Block 3.... I'd come
> to the station but the train is so often late...Don't tell anyone I
> said the hospital was casual.[24]

The nurses were over-stretched and did not get their half days off which she expected:

> My Darling Mum
> You don't know how disgusted I was when I found out I couldn't
> come out. I nearly wept with rage and disappointment! As it was
> I never got any lunch till 2.30, and I was left this afternoon to
> look after 3 wards and get ready and dispense and clean up over
> 30 teas! ... I don't think I can stand this more than a month, but
> it may be better when Matron comes back.[25]

From her few letters, it seems things did not improve:

> My darling Mum
> I don't see any chance of seeing any of you this week unless you
> come over, I was shot out of my ward on Friday at a moments
> notice over to Block I to help there. Block I at present must be
> seen to be realised. It's more like a nightmare than anything else.
> At the present moment we possess 10 absolutely helpless cases

[24]   Cheyne Collection
[25]   Ibid.

mostly acute pneumonia, bronchitis, pleurisy etc. All on 2 hrly
feeds, 4 hrly temps pulses and Resp and medicine; also everyone
has a special report book in which everything has to be noted.
You can imagine what the work is like especially, when, to ones
fevered imagination anyhow everyone wants the bedpan at least
every ten minutes and generally when the Doctor is due! To add
to our troubles yesterday two of them were absolutely raving all
day and were perpetually trying to take walks abroad round the
ward. Thank heaven we've got an orderly in last night and today
to sit and keep them in bed. I must confess they give one the
creeps when they are delirious, and I'm having enough nursing
to last me the rest of my natural life. However, I suppose we shall
get through somehow it can't last forever. Poor Matron is nearly
frantic as besides all there [sic] troubles one of the nurses a very
jolly girl [Doris Page] is fearfully bad here in the Staff House with
measles and pneumonia caught from one of the men in Block I
who is at the moment dying of it. I think she went on too long
with the measles on her and caught a chill and it's gone to her
lungs, as of course you can't catch pneumonia.

   For goodness sake come over and see me soon, as one does
want a little change when ones off. I went out to tea yesterday
and was going to the Harvey's today but can't get off. I still
survive but it's getting pretty hot and strong the sights and
sounds are — !!
Much love to Dad
Yrs in haste
Lilias[26]

There was worse to come and it is likely that it was during this period that
Lilias showed her mettle which may have contributed to her receiving the MBE
after the war.

Tuesday
Dearest Mum
Many thanks for your letter, I am getting my time off in the
mornings just these last few days so had to wire and say don't
come. I really never know when I can get off with these bad
cases, one died last night and I am afraid these others are fairly
hopeless, Doris Page is so dreadfully bad too, I believe its a very

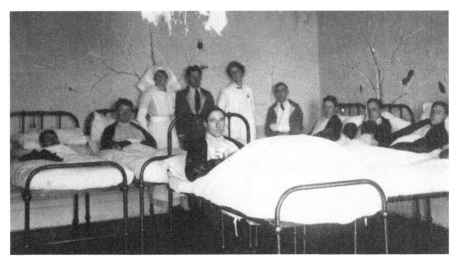

Interior of a VAD hospital ward from Lilias photograph album. Cheyne Collection

bad brand of septic-pneumonia that we've got hold of, anyhow
its getting pretty desperate. I will let you know when I have a
certain afternoon off. I'm all right except for a horrid cold, which
has made my eyes bad, I only hope they are not going to play me
the same trick they did at the Lodge, after this push is over I shall
ask matron for a day off and try to come home for a night. I don't
think I shall ever forget this week as long as I live.

Could you send me some more money, I am afraid I get
through a good deal , but washing come to about 4/- a week and
the new idea about rations leaves us a bit short sometimes, and
one has to supplement. There very often isn't enough supper to
stretch round now-a-days. If you could bring along some potted
meat when you come I'd be grateful.[27]

Doris Page did not recover; she died in February 1917 and unusually for a nurse
her name is on the Exmouth war memorial alongside the soldiers. According to notes
left on the Exmouth War Memorial website, Doris was just twenty years old when she
died and she was given a military style funeral before burial at nearby Littleham. Lilias'
letter may contain one of the few surviving comments on her illness.[28] Rider spent his
time writing a new novel which was eventually called *When the World Shook*. He also

27   Ibid. The Germans had begun using U-boats to attack supply boats bringing
      food from abroad. They were very successful at it with the result that there
      were increasing food shortages and rationing.
28   Rider was to mention Exmouth hospital years later in a reference to why Lilias
      was awarded the MBE.

continued his work with the Empire Settlement Committee and signed the report in July which he thought would be the end of his public service although he continued to sit as a magistrate in Norfolk. When he stayed at Ditchingham he could hear the guns pounding out the summer assault in Flanders. He confided in his diary that he would like to have a house in Cape Town to spend the winters of his old age.

4

Harrowing Fields

From July 27th 1917 Lilias moved to Bethnal Green Military Hospital on the Cambridge Road, London. There are no surviving letters from Lilias over this summer (perhaps Rider and/or Louie were in London) but in the Red Cross archive there are three letters from another VAD nurse known only by her signature "Flo".[1] These are from July 7th and 10th and September 28th[1]. "Flo" appears to have been from the provincial middle class and her letters are dated, detailed and measured. "Flo" described an air raid:

> We got the raid warning and had almost forgotten about it,
> when we were reminded about ¼ hr later by distant reports
> etc — which gradually grew nearer. We were in the middle of
> dressings and first went on with the work, feeling we had only
> to take chance with the rest. It seems so terrible for the poor
> boys who are so helpless, they really are nervous and try so hard
> not to show it. We saw the machines quite distinctly, I myself
> counted 28, and some of the boys who were watching all the time
> reckoned between 35 and 40.

> I had time off this afternoon and four of us went to the City by
> bus from which we had a good view of much of the damage done
> . . . the Mansion House had a near shave I believe, there were
> crowds near, in fact all over the show. The G.E. [Great Eastern]
> Rly Station caught it too.

> My room chum has been to town this evening and says the
> German trades people have been raided and rioters are very
> wild. So this is London.[2]

[1] Acc 1237/2/1, 1237/2/2, and 1237/2/3. A fourth letter is from Armistice Day, November 11th 1918 and recounts the celebrations in London. "Flo" mentions Kendal and Southport, indicating that she was from the north of England.

[2] It is possible that these letters exist in the Red Cross archive because they were never posted – being rather full of what might have been thought classified information.

A few days later "Flo" again wrote to her mother and itemised the food the nurses were eating: soup, stewed fruit, cheese, lots of honey, bread, a weekly ration of sugar, meat and fish and porridge, cocoa and good supper with two courses and cheddar cheese afterwards. She described it as plentiful but all rationed. She may, of course, have been trying to reassure her mother. "Flo" was evidently new to London and very impressed by the shops, especially Selfridges, and she had been to tea at Maison Lyons in Oxford Street where there was a big orchestra and a lady singer to entertain the diners. "Flo" then noted the friction between the regular nurses and the VADs:

> The staff nurses though are not at all fond of the VADs and I can see already that there is a bit of feeling between 'em. Our staff nurse is sarcastic to a degree and one feels sometimes like a Tommy who's got his head gardener for his officer.

"Flo"s' September letter reported more air raids:

> Our aeroplanes carry a light, and appeared like shoals of stars flitting across the sky. The flash of our guns below and in the air were very vivid — we distinctly heard the screech of two bombs. Some of the boys got the "wind up" and nurses too … I'm here to comfort the boys, when perhaps they are just wishing they had some of their own womenfolk near them. Our youngest patient is just 20 and gets very upset during a raid. He simply clung to me the other night and begged me not to leave him. He's as right as rain and as happy as a sand boy the next day.
>
>   I hope I haven't said too much in the raid line [because of censorship] expect you see it — or some of it in the paper. We smiled at Tuesday's paper which said "6 killed". Our own orderlies from the hospital ambulance alone picked up 10 killed in Shaftesbury Avenue. We heard that all the windows of the Ritz Hotel and Devonshire House were smashed.
>
>   Our last two convoys have been all South Africans, for the most part are handsome half-casts. They were held up at Dover on Monday because of a raid — the train orderlies having to go on street duty, as 40 bombs were dropped. Then they arrive here in time for another. How they all wish they'd never left home.

In his diary Rider railed about the competition between the Admiralty and the War Office that was preventing the production of enough aeroplanes to defend the country against the German Zeppelins. His nephew Andrew "who is now at government work connected with aeroplanes" told him stories of "Labour" sabotaging the work by refusing to let women do men's jobs.[3] This resentment of women taking men's jobs and — more significantly — earning men's wages was echoed in one of "Flo's" letters. Rider complained many times of the men in munitions factories in well-paid jobs, protected by unions and never called-up, yet the work could have been done by women. That same September of 1917 when the air raids were hitting London so badly, Rider sold the stock and machinery of his farm for between seven and eight thousand pounds, having decided to give up farming; he let the land at Ditchingham that he and Louie owned, but kept the house and grounds. He considered that he was well out of farming. He gave his manuscripts over to the Norwich Castle Museum. It was the end of an era. He and Louie took a flat in St Leonard's-on-Sea and one at 26 Ashley Gardens in Westminster as a London base. They had a telephone installed.

Margery Haggard in VAD uniform.
Cheyne Collection.

On October 3rd 1917 Rider transcribed a letter from his niece Margery who was nursing in a shell-shock section of Denmark Hill Hospital:

> We are seeing life all right these days; if you want excitement I recommend a "shell-shock" hospital during an air raid spell. Poor dears, they do have a bad time. You would laugh to see me going down on all fours in order to speak a few bright words to the poor things cowering under their beds. It is all pretty funny if it were not so pathetic, assuring them while you distinctly hear the whistling whirr of the shells, that "it's much further off now".

Lilias' cousin Geoff (son of Arthur) had been captured when his submarine was destroyed off the Dardanelles and he spent three and half years as a prisoner of war in Turkey. His brother Lance, an acting major in Princess Patricia's Canadian, was killed at Vimy Ridge on October 30th 1917.

Rider noted in his diary, "Soon there will be few young men of the upper classes left in England."

The letters between Lilias and her parents seem frank and open, if somewhat limited given the circumstances, but there is another witness, Harry Haggard, Alfred and Alice's eldest son, who wrote to his mother:

3   Peggy Carr, Kitty Carr's aunt, was married to Air Vice Marshall Sir Geoffrey
     Salmond, senior commander of the Royal Flying Corps.

I had an unpleasant contretemps. Dined at the Riders [in London]; he, she & Lilias there. I had heard nothing of it [Lance's death] and those queer people said not a word. At 10pm who should walk in but Uncle A. [Arthur] looking very miserable; to say when the memorial service was to be held & I had to ask what happened![4]

Why did Harry call them "those queer people"? Had death become unmentionable? Or was it because they were locked in their own tight family world?

From November 20th 1917 as the battle of Passchendaele was coming to an end Lilias was nursing at Morden Grange Auxiliary Hospital, Old Reigate Road, Betchworth in Surrey. It was a military hospital with thirty-four beds and the President of the Red Cross Committee was Lady Ashcombe with Colonel The Lord Ashcombe[5] in the chair. Lady Knowles and Mrs St Loe Strachey were on the committee. It is from the Morden Grange period that most letters survive. In terms of organisation and staff conditions it was an improvement:

> Morden Grange
> Mitcham
> Surrey
> Wednesday
> My dearest Mum
> I arrived safe and sound and am beginning to more or less know
> my way round. It is in its way a most remarkable hospital. To
> begin with you all have rooms to yourself and have not to make
> your beds or do a thing — and you are called with early tea! In
> the cottage to which I go on Friday one is allowed a fire in either
> one or the other of the Pro's [professional nurses' rooms] it is
> all right and will tell you more when I see you don't expect many
> letters as time is not over plentiful but you get a little more than
> 2hrs as meal times are not counted in fact if you have the aft
> [afternoon off] you get quite three which I have this afternoon.
> Much love — show this to Dad and give him my best love — note
> the address. I gave it you wrong.
> Yrs always

---

4   Letter in the Lyster Collection from Vernon Harry Stuart Haggard (1874–1960), a career naval officer, he was awarded the *Croix de Guerre* in 1919. Later he became 4th Sea Lord and was promoted to admiral, KCMG and CMB.
5   Baron Ashcombe of Dorking was a Cubitt, originally a Norfolk family who made their fortune from building development in London.

Lilias

PS Hope yr throat is all right.[6]

The nursing, however, was relentless. If Lilias had a reputation for clumsiness, one can also surmise from this letter that at least her cheerfulness was welcome:

> You would laugh if you could see my true position in this
> establishment. Its rather like that of the Cap and bells at Court
> and likewise carries various privileges for some reason I've
> captured a corner of Sister's somewhat erratic affections and
> therefore when I fall violently into the various scrapes that beset
> the path of the unwary in hospital, which I do on an average
> about once a week
> she merely tries
> to look severe and
> ends by remarking
> "only Haggard again
> I suppose" and
> beaming upon me.
> May it only last until
> I depart! I smashed
> a man's EX [Sic]
> Ray plate to atoms
> yesterday, luckily it wasn't his last one — and she didn't mind a
> bit, although its true the beastly thing split clear in half of itself.[7]

Interior of a ward at Morden Grange VAD hospital.
Cheyne Collection

She also still struggled with the night shifts:

> My little expedition to London with Hughie came to grief
> as instead of going out I was stretched out with a rotten bad
> head feeling like nothing on earth and had to send him a wire
> and stay in bed till 12 tonight which was a sad end to my little
> dissipations! The fact is I'd had practically no sleep for two days
> and when you have to go on like that it does one in completely
> and I felt extremely sorry for my little self and as if I "wanted my
> Mummy" very very badly. However perhaps things will improve
> in time. I started off quite gaily and thought I was going to be
> quite a dab at this game but there's been a sad falling off![8]

6   Cheyne Collection.
7   Ibid, undated.
8   Ibid, undated. Hughie Scudamore, son of the vicar at Ditchingham – Lilias
     planned several outings with him.

Her occasionally infantile style of writing erupted again when she wrote to her father:

> My dearest Daddy
> Do write to me sometimes, I get hurt in my little feelings when
> you forget all about me, though I know you sometimes think
> I haven't got any! I believe you're afraid I shall write to you
> medical details. I am sorry if they slip into once letters but you
> see they are one's whole life and interest here, and it's difficult
> not to talk about them as a matter of fact. I know you are busy so
> don't take me seriously![1]

While there are still traces of the rather gung-ho girl in these letters, another more serious tone is emerging— that of a seasoned nurse:

> Morden Grange Hospital
> Mitcham Surrey
> Wednesday mrg
> My dearest Mum
> Many thanks for your letter which I should have answered before
> only we have been so busy. We had a fearsome flap on Sunday
> 14 hrs in the theatre and 16 poor victims cut up, just as Captain
> Turner and Dr Passmore were going at about 10pm one of the
> "stumps" started haemorrhaging so appallingly that, after vain
> efforts to stop it Sister sent me flying to stop the Drs and the
> wretched boy was sent back into the theatre and the whole "op"
> had to be done again and then didn't get out till nearly midnight.
> As you can imagine we had a night of it especially as three or
> four of them were pretty bad afterwards and still are poor dears,
> some of these unfortunate men go through absolute hell with
> there [sic] stumps. Nine or ten operations, and the most dreadful
> pain, Hal[2] can never realise what he escaped.[3]

To counter the stress Lilias tried to make sure that she got up to London on her days off, or visited her parents in St Leonards if they were not at their London flat.

> I shall be going up to Town on Friday and take my things down
> to the Club[4] and change there I think it will be better than the

[1]   Cheyne Collection.
[2]   Cousin Hal, son of Will, had his leg amputated below the knee.
[3]   Cheyne Collection.
[4]   In other letters Lilias mentions The Albermarle Club, Dover Street and the
      University Club. Kitty Carr belonged to the University Club.

other plan. I really can't go up to lunch and a matinee I should
be too dead now we are having such busy nights ...[5]

Without proper training all Lilias could do was to learn on the job and she was
pleased to receive approval from the regular nurses...

> ...much to my disgust there was so much to do buzzing round I
> had no chance to watch the "ops", we were all fairly tired as one
> case turned out to be much worse than we expected and they
> had to do a tremendous short circuit operation, which took more
> than two hours. I was awfully sick I didn't get a chance to see it,
> as I was furiously washing up and boiling instruments and gloves
> just outside and spending my spare moments with the people
> who were coming round! However Sister told me this morning
> I've got to go up to "theatre Ward" with the Staff Nurse as the
> theatre Pro' [professional nurse] is wasted downstairs which is a
> small feather in my cap quite a small one, but still a feather....[6]

Although Lilias' letters contain little comment on the progress of the war she
noted the effects of the Allied attacks and the counter-attacks on the casualties
and the increasing food shortages:

> ... we [the nurses] are cutting down our meat tremendously
> here and lots of them won't eat it more than once a day — even
> if it's on the table and one can get along all right if times are not
> too strenuous I find, anyhow.[7]

Bread was being heavily subsidised by the government to the tune of £40
million - a policy which Rider commented on in his diaries as storing up
problems of debt for the future. There were more immediate problems amongst
the desperately poor:

> M. G. H.
> Jan 26th 1918
> My dearest Mum,
> You really do seem to be having an awful time over the food
> question. We are all right here although they say there was
> rioting in Wimbledon tonight and we heard that all the soldiers
> on Wimbledon Common have got to "stand to" tonight because
> of it. I really am not surprised as I went up to London early

5   Cheyne Collection.
6   Ibid.
7   Ibid.

Friday morning and the whole way up through the poorer parts
the streets were filled with literally hundreds of people standing
in queues outside every butchers and margarine shop it really
looked awful, and is as if the population were starving. …
I still survive and am cheered by the discovery that I come off
night duty on Feb 11th and have a weeks holiday as they are
going to count the week I did before and I therefore have only to
do five for which Heaven be praised!

When next you see me don't be surprised if I appear completely
soft — the mental rot that sets in with night duty is positively
paralysing one does nothing but sleep and eat and occasionally
in a wild fit of energy make some undies,
Your ever loving
Lilias
Lilias [sic][8]

The week's holiday obviously
materialised since Rider noted in his
diary on February 18th that "I hear
from Lilias today that the food supplied
at breakfast at the Dover Street Hotel
where she and her mother are staying
was so insufficient that they had to retire
to their rooms and eat potted meat and
biscuits!" Lilias also told him that she
had heard of officers attached to their
home mess enjoying lavish foods of all
kinds.[9]

Several of Lilias' female cousins had
also been doing war work and, like
Lilias, weathered the awful experience.
Her sister Angie, a gentle placid

Lilias in VAD uniform. Cheyne Collection.

character, was not really strong enough for the strain. Nevertheless she did what
she could; her husband Tom was a temporary medical officer in the army. What
Lilias missed most was the country life she had been used to.

8   Cheyne Collection.
9   In an October 15th 1918 entry in his diary Rider, on a trip to Wales, noted there
     was no rationing or shortages there; he surmised that the miners would not
     put up with it and the government would not risk their adverse reaction.

On February 1st 1918 she wrote to her father:

> ... The part of hospital I hate the most is always being indoors
> you do absolutely long to get more air and exercise.
>   We have had two lively nights lately — the old Morden gun
> fairly surpassed herself and fired 270 rounds the first night,
> the din was fearsome and all the men upstairs had to sleep on
> the floor down below except one poor dear who was too ill to
> be moved! But luckily he didn't mind a scrap. The only result
> of all the energy is we have had nearly half the gun crew in as
> casualties, with contured (?) and broken fingers and colic from
> chill etc, ... [10]

Many years later Lilias was to recount in *Norfolk Life* a more distilled version
of the events of that night:

> Soon the persistent whine and drone of aeroplanes dug me
> out of my bed, to see a little cluster of stars drifting across a
> faintly translucent sky, pursued by the sweeping fingers of the
> searchlights, and the dull whump whump of anti-aircraft guns.
> A sound that never fails to take me back to the spring of 1918, a
> hospital just outside London in the path of the German raiders,
> and a particular Sunday which remains grimly in my memory.
> We had had eighteen operations, in most of which I had been a
> not too enthusiastic participant; I had endured that nightmare
> of the amateur nurse, a slipped ligature on a main artery; I had
> had a wigging from Sister for speaking to the visiting surgeon
> who happened to be friend of my brother-in-law's;[11] and at
> nine o'clock was finishing my ministrations to the unfortunate
> theatre victims, and tottering towards bed, when we had an air
> raid warning, the fifth in a week. It was the last straw. Down on
> stretchers had to come every man who was "moveable", and I
> was left with the half dozen who were not, in a dimly-lit ward
> with the planes droning overhead, and the whack and thump of
> the anti-aircraft gun in the garden, feeling I did not care if forty
> bombs dropped on me or anyone else as long as I never saw a
> hospital again and could go to bed for a month! A whisper came
> from a bed near me (a long brown New Zealander so ill that

[10]   Cheyne Collection.
[11]   Tom Haggard, Angie's husband.

the hard-driven surgeon, seeing his mangled body on the table, exclaimed: "What the hell are you wasting my time for — he'll die," and proceeded at once to do his utmost, as it turned out, successfully): "Please go downstairs, nurse; I don't mind dying alone; I heard what the doc said — and it's safer downstairs." All my life I shall remember how ashamed I felt of my mental backsliding, when faced with that fortitude.[12]

After that awful night she wrote perhaps the most telling passage in all her letters. Referring to their family casualties she says:

The cousins are getting decidedly broken up [i.e. so many have died] — I always think no one need mind "going over" now would [be] going[in] such good company, what ever is over the other side anyhow they are there too. And there are so many of them now. There is a horrible calendar hangs over at the cottage we always tease the girl who bought it which has "life is meant for work and not for care, for strivings and not Happiness" or some such unpleasant sentiment on it, but much cogitation the last few months have convinced me that its true, anyhow now-a-days, but perhaps I may be feeling pessimistic after too much night duty! But to see the wrecks of men who have got to live their lives out somehow maimed and broken in every way is enough to make anyone pessimistic occasionally.[13]

When she did manage to get some holiday she returned to the concerns and rhythms of her upper middle class. In a letter of May 10th 1918 when she was staying at her parents' flat at 26 Ashley Gardens; to her mother she writes of supplying accounts for her allowance, buying clothes for the summer:

I enclose the accounts up to date since I last sent it to you. I think it's for about a fortnight — or a little more, clothes are getting absolutely too appallingly expensive for words. I've bought one new hat, some gloves, stockings and my one extravagance too [sic] voile frocks ...

She and Angie were taking driving lessons: "I had my first driving lesson today and didn't kill anyone! They put you first on a huge ambulance run by gas and take you round and round Berkley Square." A friend or acquaintance was urging them to go out to France with a fleet of 20 ambulances but there was a hitch:

---

[12]   *Norfolk Life* (London: Faber and Faber, 1946), 173.
[13]   Letter dated February 1st 1918, Cheyne Collection.

Unfortunately it's run by Lady Angela Forbes[14] so its out of the question to get tarred with that brush tho' Angie was dead keen because it's a chance she may not get again as she can't go to the English Army and anyhow it's not easy to get out now at all. However, I am afraid it's out of the question. Aunt Judy nearly had a fit and said she should come down to St Leonard's at once to protest![15]

Lady Angela Forbes was a daughter of the Earl of Rosslyn and half-sister to Daisy Warwick, who had been a mistress to Edward VII. Her sister was married to the Duke of Sutherland. Lady Angela had been divorced from her husband, James Forbes the premier baron of Scotland, since 1907 and had become the mistress of Lord Elcho, heir to Lord Wemyss. Elcho

Amputees at Morden Grange. Cheyne Collection.

was a founder member of The Souls, a social and intellectual elite, who preferred the cultural atmosphere of a *salon* to political debate. Almost from the start of the war Lady Angela organised catering facilities at the railway stations in London to meet every train bringing home troops from the Front. They were known as "angelinas". She was the very first "Forces Sweeheart". Despite what appears to be a generous contribution to the war effort with practical support for the soldiers, and despite her high social standing, her reputation was irrevocably tarred by her advanced sexual views and behaviour. The Haggards remained steadfastly Victorian in their social mores.

Rider's diaries give vent to his feelings about Germany, Russia and the future of Europe: he predicted a second war within thirty years. While he never intended them to be published in his lifetime he did share some of his political comments with a Norwich-born socialist writer and Labour Party politician, James "Fred" Henderson, who asked permission to quote a passage in the *Eastern Daily Press*. Henderson had sent Rider a copy of his book *The New Faith: A Study of Party Politics and the War*; the pernicious effects of party politics were one of Rider's bugbears. Even though he and Henderson came from different ends of the social and political spectrum Rider's letters of 1918 show that when it came to actual

14   Lady Angela Forbes (1876-1950) was born Lady Angelina Selina Bianca St Clair-Erskine.
15   Cheyne Collection.

policies and attitudes they had much in common and mutual respect.

Early in March 1918 speculations about the fate of the Romanovs began to filter through to England. Rider had already expressed his poor view of the weak character of the Czar in his diary; it was believed that "Nicky" had made a pact with his cousin the Kaiser as far back as 1904 with a view to bringing Britain down. Rider heard again from his friend Teddy Roosevelt who regretted that America had not joined the war two years previously. Ill-health forced Rider to retire from his latest Commission and he went down to St Leonard's to nurse his weak chest.

Back in Norfolk Will Haggard, Rider's eldest brother, sold up the family home, West Bradenham Hall. For Will, as a retired diplomat who had spent all his working life abroad, there were few attractions to rural isolation; the estate needed repair and upkeep while the farms brought in little or no income. Rider noted that these estates, which were once an integrated part of the rural economy, were now only viable for the very rich. Rider said good-bye to all his youthful memories and later went to the sale of the contents to buy back some of the items which had the most sentimental value for him. With fuel prices rising Rider shut down the last of his orchid houses at Ditchingham bringing to a close the hobby that had given him so much pleasure.

A group of army officers at The Red House, Mettingham with Lilias centre front looking down. Sir John Twigg is in the back row, second from right. Cheyne Collection.

Lilias' last months of nursing were spent close to home at The Red House in Mettingham, the home of Sir John Twigg, a retired Indian civil servant and his wife Lady Twigg who organised the VAD convalescent accommodation for colonial soldiers. According to Lilias, Lady Twigg much appreciated her help and her car. Lilias had evidently taken enthusiastically to driving and joked that the car was probably much more useful than she was. Since Mettingham is just east of Bungay and only a couple of miles from Ditchingham, letters were unnecessary except to her father while he was away. In one of these she told Rider the stories of German cruelties to prisoners of war which had been recounted to her. By mid-summer 1918 the influenza epidemic was in full swing and many members of the Carr family at Ditchingham Hall fell ill, although not fatally.

Rider's entry in his diary for July 5th 1918 read:

> The influenza outbreak, the Spanish sickness as it is called, is growing very bad indeed. Tom, who himself is a sufferer at the front, writes that he has seen men fall down with it suddenly as though they were shot, and one hears much the same in other quarters.

The summer was hot and the water pump at Mettingham was not working. As usual Lilias coped and made light of the difficulties. For respite she brought some of the servicemen home to Ditchingham and had a particular fondness for the Australians.

Lilias in her car called 'Susan Jane'. Cheyne Collection.

One of the Australian soldiers.
Cheyne Collection.

Paradoxically, in some ways Rider felt vindicated by the war; he had felt out of tune with the Victorian age and its emphasis on trade and materialism. In his view Victorians were only interested in money and had time neither for the high-minded aims of Empire nor for spiritual aspirations. He thought that a "virile fighting spirit" was necessary to combat "the yoke of slavery and ultimate destruction".[16]

As Alison Light pointed out in *Forever England*,

It was perfectly possible, as Vera Brittain's account of her sufferings in *Testament of Youth* makes clear, for those who had lost their loved ones to learn to hate war and yet keep the romantic image of the heroic sacrifice of individuals untarnished; indeed it may have been the only way to cope with the trauma of their loss, as well as offering a felt tribute to the idealism which the war destroyed. Trauma provokes conservative as well as radical responses.[17]

In the autumn Rider retreated to St Leonard's; he bemoaned the paper shortages that kept his back list of novels out of print and the reduction in royalties because publishers were unable to turn a profit. In October he noted that there was a certain feeling in the air that the war might end soon and on November 11th it did. Rider wrote:

Never more will the ex-Kaiser, never more will any monarch, as I believe, be able to arrogate to himself a flesh different to the herd of men, or flaunt the banner of a Right Divine in the faces of the struggling people.[18]

He went down to Batemans to spend time with Kipling, for many years his most intimate friend. In the King's New Year's Honours List of 1919 Rider was awarded a KBE — Knight of the British Empire.

---

[16]   *The War Diaries of H. Rider Haggard*, July 5th 1918, typed transcript Volume 10, pages not numbered.

[17]   Alison Light, *Forever England*, (London: Routledge, 1991), 200.

[18]   *The War Diaries of H. Rider Haggard*, November 10th 1918 , typed transcript Volume XI, pages not numbered.

Lilias had already officially left the VAD but she continued her work at Mettingham with colonial casualties and influenza victims and then gradually returned to civilian life. In a letter written from "Hillride" where she was staying with Muriel Turner and her child she responded to Rider's account of a sumptuous public dinner in London with an amusing anecdote about the rationing and food shortages that were still the order of the day for most people. She told him that she was becoming more domesticated with regard to cooking and also wrote about the hopeless employment prospects for so many of the young men returning from the war — some of whom had never known anything but the army.

Among her papers are several letters (written very properly to "Miss Haggard") from an Australian engineer named H. J. Stone who had been at the Red House and who evidently retained a fondness for her and her family. In a shy, restrained way he seemed quite smitten with Lilias and he obviously would have liked to stay in England if his future prospects had not been tied up with his training as an engineer and a career back in Melbourne. The last letter reported his engagement to an Australian girl and his ambition to work in America. Another favourite was Bill Lyndhurst from South Australia whose photo appeared several times in her album and years later she recalled that she had been romantically involved with an Australian in the spring of 1919.[19]

In the New Year's honours list for 1920 Lilias was awarded the War Service Bar and MBE for her nursing work. It was a focus of attention which, like the camera, she found unwelcome. Worse still she worried that it might have been awarded at the prompting of her father. Her father wrote to her from North Lodge, St Leonard's-on-Sea on January 22nd:

> My dearest Lilias
>
>   Bear up! We all meet with what you call "Cadomas" sometimes! I don't think I am the wicked cause of your misfortunes. Only in a speech I made distributing the Red Cross badges for [unreadable] without mentioning names I spoke of the Exmouth business[20] and a swell who, unknown to me, was on the platform afterwards asked particulars, but said he would not quote the matter as it would involve stirring up dirty waters.
> You may remember the names I suggested but yours was not one of them; indeed you being my daughter I should not have done so.

[19]   Letter to Margaret Spurrell in the Cheyne collection, when Lilias was turning out Ditchingham House and found old letters.

[20]   This may have been the outbreak of measles that killed Doris Page or simply the shortage of staff and poor organisation.

For the rest my dear, I think you have quite deserved the
little distinction though that is not saying that others have
not deserved it also. I hope you filled up and returned the
form properly. One must never decline these things: it is the
unforgiveable sin. No time for more dear as I am only just back
from Town where I went for the dinner to the Prince.
With all suitable condolences
Believe me dearest your loving father
H. Rider Haggard[21]

Their easy companionship continued and Lilias went on several fishing
trips to Wales and Scotland with her father and his new friend Sir Ronald Ross
(1857–1932), an Indian-born doctor who had won the Nobel Prize for his work
on connecting mosquitoes with malaria. Ross was also an author of adventure
novels which may have been where his interests crossed with Rider's.

Several of Rider's stories were translated into the quickly developing medium
of films which brought in a new income and wider fame for him. Profiteers had
done well out of the war and vulgarly displayed their wealth in a country where
vast numbers of people were out of work, impoverished and damaged by the war.
Rider noted an atmosphere of restlessness and vacuity among the young. The
jazz age had arrived. There was also unprecedented social flux that undermined
the notion of service, deference and class.

Lilias, aged 28, sank back into her beloved countryside and in 1921 organised
her first local country fair on the lawns at Ditchingham House. It was a Fur,
Feather and Vegetable Show with Rider as the "President" and became an annual
fixture in south Norfolk. This small initiative is rather telling in that Lilias is
embedding herself in her childhood Ditchingham life and calling on her father's
patronage. Meanwhile Lilias' contemporaries were wrestling with adult life. Her
friend Kitty Carr, already a mother, discovered that she did not love her husband
and embarked on a passionate affair with one of his fellow officers. Kitty's sister
Peggy "told" on her which must have caused a considerable stir among their
social circle at Ditchingham. However, divorce was unthinkable not least because
under the legislation of the time she would lose her children. Kitty's marriage,
now openly unhappy, continued.[22] This can scarcely have been encouraging to
Lilias but there is no particular indication that Lilias was looking for a husband.

Rider continued to comment on international affairs in his diary: August 10
th1922 "the truth is that all Europe is threatened with bankruptcy, and we shall be
lucky if we are not dragged into the vortex…. I think too that it is she (Germany)

21   Cheyne Collection.
22   Diana Athill, *Life Class*, 106/107.

who has really won the war, inasmuch as she has half ruined the rest of the world, while remaining internally fairly prosperous herself, also quite undevastated." His niece Margery Charlton was the wife of the British Consul General in Berlin and wrote to him with a contradictory view about the dreadful poverty being caused in Germany by the weak exchange rate: "It's a great pity they (the Germans) didn't get their Moratorium [on their debts] but obviously the French don't want them to pay — they want the Ruhr."

In England agriculture, after a short post-war boom, slid into a dire state. The government had provided, via county council purchases of farms which were then sub-divided, for smallholdings to be taken up by ex-servicemen with the help of government bank loans. They were not economically viable units and many people saw it as a waste of tax payers' money. The depletion of estate capital by death duties and the security of tenure enjoyed by inefficient tenant farmers contributed to the slump. The Corn Protection Acts had been repealed and there was free import of food; farm wages and farm earnings were low.

With the signing of the Treaty of Versailles in 1921 the war was officially over. Rider's eldest and much loved sister Ella died the same year. In September the Walker Art Gallery in Liverpool advertised the exhibition of a portrait of Rider by Maurice Grieffenhagen. Lilias accompanied him to the opening as she did on many expeditions and social occasions including the 1922 Buckingham Palace garden party where Rider met many old friends including Rudyard Kipling. At

An army officer in one of the Haggard cars — an Hispano-Suiza. Cheyne Collection

the Athanaeum those who were attending the party placed bets on who was wearing the oldest frock coat; Rider thought his was Victorian.

In November 1922, Howard Carter, who had been raised in Swaffham, Norfolk, and whom Rider already knew, made an outstanding and marvellous discovery in the Valley of the Kings at Thebes. Carter, in the employ of Lord Carnarvon, had opened up the burial chambers of Tutankhamun.

5

Father Lands

In January of 1924, Rider, aged 67 and in failing health, set out for a restorative trip to Egypt. Accompanying him was Lilias who, aged 31, was now recognised by family and friends to be Rider's "inseparable companion". Also in the party was Rider's niece Joan Haggard aged 34 (daughter of Aggie and his deceased brother Jack) and Helena Rotenberg, a middle-aged matron and family friend. Louie was taking a separate holiday in France.

In mid-January they crossed the Bay of Biscay heading for Marseilles via Gibraltar. The weather was bad with heavy seas and cold winds. Joan suffered from sea-sickness but she amused Rider and everyone else with her lively banter. Rider wrote to his wife: "She groaned and moaned and blamed Lilias for bringing her by longsea [sic]".

"A little more firmness and I might have gone overland," Joan had sighed.

It was unlikely that any firmness from Joan would have outweighed other considerations. The sea voyage had been chosen particularly in the hope of providing a bracing and restorative environment for Rider. Lilias recalled many years later that Rider's "spirits rose with every day they travelled eastwards. Anxieties and depressions were laid aside, his health improved, and he became an extraordinarily amusing companion. He had a great interest in his fellow man and vast sense of kindly humour, which exercised itself gaily upon all the accidents of travel and the foibles of his fellow travellers."

This trip to Egypt was not simply to see the antiquities so recently augmented by Howard Carter's discovery of Tutankhamun's tomb; although that alone would be an exciting prospect. For Rider there was a semi-mystical aspect to the expedition. He knew he was not a well man and writing to an old friend he speculated about which of them would die first. All his life he had been fascinated by the idea of reincarnation and how it fitted in with the Christian concept of the after life. A mystic had told him that he had had several incarnations, twice in ancient Egypt, once as a minor Pharaoh. In his autobiography, *The Days of My Life*, he admitted to veneration for Isis and said he always felt inclined to bow to the moon. Like many Victorians, he was also fascinated by his genealogy. By visiting Egypt there was a sense in which he would be returning home, communing with his ancestors.

A man who believes in reincarnation enlarges his scale of reference. Certainly the detail of Rider's many novels set in ancient Egypt convinced his readers that he had an uncanny knowledge of life under the Pharaohs.[1] Rider's writing-style had a suitably impressive Old Testament flavour, the result, no doubt, of his familiarity with the King James Bible and the Book of Common Prayer.

Reincarnated or not, Rider was rather larger than life: highly-strung, suffering from poor digestion and very disorganised.

Lilias said that

> Rider was never known to travel anywhere without losing
> his luggage. It was always in vast quantity, colossal in weight,
> and generally composed of the solid skins of crocodiles and
> such like reptiles. Whether its exotic appearance attracted the
> luggage thief, or the initials H.R.H. deluded them into thinking
> it contained the possessions of royalty and vast rewards would
> be theirs for returning it, no one ever knew. The fact remains, it
> was always lost, and the myrmidons of Messrs. Cook, faint but
> pursuing, chased it up and down the globe… [2]

After his death Helena Meade of Earsham Hall, a Ditchingham neighbour, wrote to Lilias commenting, "you can always look back on what a help and comfort you have been to him — and of how much you were always able to help him".[3] On this occasion the luggage seems to have been less of an issue, at least until the time for packing-up on the way back. On the voyage out, Joan and Lilias shared quarters and Joan protested that Lilias "ramps about the cabin like a young tornado". Rider added "the row when they are both talking in it (the cabin) is considerable". One might be forgiven for thinking of them as young girls not long out of school but by the standards of the time their mature age and unmarried state made them very much spinsters.

By January 22nd, Rider reported to his wife that they were off Port Said from where they would travel by train to Cairo. The skies were dull and wet and the

---

1   *Cleopatra* 1889, *The Way of the Spirit* 1906, *Morning Star* 1910, *Smith and the Pharaohs* 1920, *Queen of the Dawn*, 1925 (April).
2   *The Cloak that I Left*, 131.
3   Letter of condolence in the Cheyne Collection.

temperature remained cold. Rider gave four lectures to his fellow passengers on the history of Egypt as part of a contract with the P&O shipping line. He remarked with typical wryness that these lectures had met with considerable success, "at least they all seemed pleased with my artless efforts — knowing even less about the subject than I do myself!" Lilias asked her father to send her love to her mother: she would not be writing as she had nothing to say.

At Port Said they were joined by Percy Calvert who was related by marriage to Rider's youngest brother Major Edward Arthur Haggard. Ralph Calvert and some other tourists also appeared but whether here or slightly later is not clear. Lilias recalled later that "with a daughter, a nephew, a niece and various old friends in the party, even he [Rider] could not suffer from homesickness".

A dust storm hindered their progress to Cairo and they did not arrive at the Continental Hotel in the Place de l'Opéra until late afternoon. An agent, a Mr Tadros, met them and helped them through customs. The very next morning they set off for the Nile steamer, the SS *Victoria*. Along the way they were joined by Geoffrey Haggard and his new wife "Mardie" (Margery Syme) fresh from their honeymoon in Naples.[4] Geoffrey, apparently, was good company but his bride was sullenly silent; Rider thought she would open up in time.

Five days later, by January 27th, they had sailed upstream and arrived at Assiout Barrage. According to Lilias: "The whole party went up the Nile by boat, spending long days visiting tombs and temples, riding over the desert, inspecting recent excavations at Sakkara and Assuit and so up to Luxor."

Lilias was to write later of one curious incident that occurred when a fortune teller came aboard and told fortunes to the chattering travellers. Far from being a disbeliever, Rider recalled the Zulu witch doctors he had come across in Africa whose divinations were mediated through "bones". When it came to his nephew Geoffrey's turn Rider advised him: "leave the man alone, my boy — you may hear something you don't like." The Arab caught the discouraging tone of voice but did not understand the kindly meaning of Rider's words and looked hard at Rider and said in a low voice, "You call me a common cheat — is it not so? — Then what of the son of whom you always think?" Again, according to Lilias, only she and her father heard this remark. It cut sharply to the core of Rider's melancholy.

Lilias was enjoying herself but complained about not being able to eat the salads (for fear of food poisoning) and about the price of bottled water. The weather was warming up and they planned to go ashore for the day. Lilias was beginning to take photographs. Three days on they arrived at Luxor where they planned to spend several days before moving on to Aswan. The nights were still near freezing

---

4   Geoffrey had been a prisoner-of-war in Turkey and was son of Arthur Haggard.

The Haggard party in Egypt; Rider and Lilias sitting front row centre. Cheyne Collection.

although the days were improving. Rider was hoping to make advance bookings in the old Luxor Hotel so that they could return there by train from Cairo later in their holiday. There were various combinations of friends who might join them. A donkey ride to Abydos had shaken Rider's spine and caused Percy Calvert painful injuries to his backside. Lilias and Joan complained of the lack of chocolate and English tea. "It is marvellous how dependent English young women are upon

Rider and one of the women of the party, possibly Lilias, on donkeys.
Cheyne Collection.

their afternoon tea and sweets." Mardie had not opened-up but continued so silent that Percy Calvert had given up trying to talk to her at all.

On February 1st they began their expedition to visit the Valley of the Kings. Rider and Lilias, alone of the party, had received an invitation from Howard Carter to enter "Tut's tomb". Carter, like Rider, had been inspired by the Amherst's huge collection of Egyptian artefacts at Didlington Hall; Carter had also been financed initially by the Amhersts. Rider went by donkey but Lilias and the saddle-sore Percy Calvert went by carriage. It was a long and tiring day with endless climbing of steps into tombs and views of Colossi and temples. Rider remarked that Lilias didn't seem to have "brought back any clear impressions of the last few temples and no wonder for the mind can only absorb a certain amount in a given time". One of their fellow tourists, Maud Gross of Woodbridge, noted Rider's attention to Lilias:

> I remember when in Egypt if there was anything special or of
> marked interest Sir Rider always called to you — waited — and
> did not move on till you had seen it. A small thing — but it is
> those little things that show so much and told one how much you
> were to him.[5]

Howard Carter's secretary Mr Bethele conducted Rider and Lilias into Tutankhamen's tomb. The other members of the party stood at the top of the steps and enviously photographed them going in and out. Inside Rider and Lilias found a worn and tired Mr Carter "doing something with wedges". The tomb in itself was "small and rather disappointing" — so much had been removed or was covered in sacking awaiting removal. Rider remarked on the continuing row between Carter and the Egyptian government and noted that Lilias was one of the very few women who had been allowed in the tomb.

Lilias was very taken with Luxor and the weather was now mild without being too hot. She and Rider planned to return later in the month and then go on to Palestine with Joan. Their next stop was the islands of Philae which Rider remembered wistfully as covered in temples and monuments, many

At the entrance to a tomb — since it is the only picture of this subject it is probably the tomb of Tutankhamun. Cheyne Collection.

5   Letter of condolence in the Cheyne Collection.

dedicated to the goddess Isis, built in the Ptolemaic period about 350 BC; with the demise of the old Egyptian gods they were abandoned and later still defaced by Christians. The building of the Aswan Dam in 1902 and its expansion after 1907 led to the submergence of the islands. Lilias nearly frightened the life out of her father by "calmly marching along the granite parapet waving a camera with a kind of Niagara 140 feet below her." Although she came back safely, Rider reported that he was nearly sick.

By now Mardie was proving herself a complete "wet-blanket" who took no interest in anything and barely talked with anyone except occasionally with Joan. She expressed a wish to join up with her mother who was staying at Port Said (perhaps in transit to some other part of the Empire) but her new husband did not wish to expend the money. One imagines that an upper middle class girl on her honeymoon in the 1930s might indeed wish to talk to her mother. But no one seems to have thought of what discomfort she might be experiencing although Rider commented "she is but a child and quite uneducated and it may all come out right in the end — if she has children".

There were further complications when Helen Rotenberg, who did not get on with a certain Miss Samuel, felt left out of the planned return trip to Luxor. The misunderstanding was sorted out eventually but not without resentment from Joan who had expected Helen to accompany her for a week in Palestine. Rider remarked

Rider with one of the women of the party, heavily veiled against the dust. Cheyne Collection.

with resignation, "Women are very odd fish!"

By the 8th February Rider and Lilias had decided that a trip to Palestine would be too costly and they would be better off at Luxor with perhaps a few days at the Mena House Hotel next to the pyramids. Rider noted that very few English people could afford these trips anymore and most of their travelling companions are Americans, Austrians, Argentines, French and Jews. Lilias took a second visit to the temple at Denderah and like Percy suffered from a sore behind from riding a donkey. As they moved north they came into chillier weather and Rider was glad to return to Cairo. Percy Calvert had a cold and bronchitis.

Rider was not the only one who was glad to see Cairo. The younger members of the party were looking for more excitement than tombs and temples. The very first evening Joan and Geoff dragged Mardie out to the Cairo Music Hall and did not get back until 2am. The next night they went off again to a dance at a hotel. Joan had joined up with an army officer, George, whom she had known in England and they dined together every evening and went off to dances and a night club afterwards – Joan was irritated that Lilias would not join them. Both Geoff and Joan were "never still". Rider was beginning to take a more jaundiced view of the younger generation. Mardie he found "just a child who has been spoilt and is naturally lazy and taciturn. But underneath she has quick perceptions and she is very fond of Geoff who she irritates considerably. Also she has a sense of humour. She said goodbye to me with a good deal of affection last night, embracing me warmly – although she has scarcely spoken to me on the voyage. A queer child! Geoff too is queer – like most of our breed. A most attractive chap – but he can't stop still! Nor can Joan." Of this niece whom he found so amusing at the beginning of the trip, he now notes, "For her life is one long 'scream' yet she is awfully clever and does a load of work. "

Unlike her cousin, Lilias preferred to be out of Cairo. The party that would return to Luxor was Rider, Lilias, Helen Rotenberg and Miss Evelyn Samuel. A Miss Lowther whom they both liked (although she had spots as a result of taking bromide continually) was to join them. Rider was grateful for Helen's help with the packing – "she don't argue like Lilias, but just packs like the devil". While Helen and Lilias packed, Rider spent the morning at the Museum looking at the "Tut. things". Later he learned that Geoff and Joan had not returned to the hotel until three in the morning and had to be up at 5am.

Two days later they were still in Cairo, Rider and Lilias having been to the opera to see *Aida*, and Rider's patience with the ambience of Cairo and with the younger generation was wearing thin.

> This place to my mind is simply horrible and I detest it. If
> you could see the cosmopolitan mobs in this caravanserai:
> the old hags hung round with jewels, the ladies painted to
> resemble women of the street, the American females, some of
> them dressed in breeches without a skirt, the fat Greeks, the
> oleaginous Egyptians and Levantines, all pursuing Life as they
> understand it! Then there are the dust (which does my throat
> no good) and the screaming motor horns and the wretches who
> hang round you like flies all intent of extracting money as soon

as you step out of doors. However to a generation which I think, lacks the repose and dignity of that which preceded it, all this acceptable enough. If Life is "one long, long scream", well, that's how they like it!

It was fortunate that Lilias was able to counter-balance his irritation with her own humour. At one point Joan was so restless that Rider considered her on the point of breakdown. She had fallen out with Miss Samuel who was chasing Ralph Calvert. Joan's friend George unwisely took up with Miss Samuel while Joan was at the races. Lilias was in hysterics of laughter when she recounted the story of Joan's subsequent explosion when she found out. But this was not the end of Rider's troubles with women. When Miss Evelyn Samuel took Joan's place next to Rider at the dinner table, Joan lashed out at her verbally and later abused her to everyone else in the party. Rider said Joan was as venomous with her tongue as her father (Jack) had been, and also coarse and vulgar, using swear words. Meanwhile Miss Samuel continued to pursue Ralph Calvert and anyone else in trousers — Rider feared for an Australian acquaintance, Mr Crosse, who was due to join them. "These women are so different to what women used to be — of romance there is none, of other things too much. Dignity too is utterly lacking."

On February 14th Geoff and Mardie departed for Ceylon and married life in the colonies. Percy Calvert and Joan had moved off to Palestine. Rider and Lilias and their small party headed for Luxor, arriving on the 19th February. A few days later Lilias came down with the 'flu and was confined to her room for three days. It was during this quiet period that Rider "had leisure to sit in the sun and dream." He wrote in his diary:

> Sometimes it is possible to sit alone in some hall of the great temples as I did today. I looked about me in silence which was broken only by the hum of bees who hive upon the walls, and the twitter of the building birds. Everywhere soared great columns as firmly set as when they were built; upon sculptured walls where Kings made offerings to painted gods, or goddesses led them by the hand into some holy presence. Here was the place where for tens of centuries priests marched from sanctuary to sanctuary following the order of their ritual; where proud Pharaoh, himself a god, bent the knee before other gods, whose company he soon must join, and received from them all blessings and the gift of life for thousands and thousands of years. Surely such a spot should be holy if there is aught so on earth? Yet see — there the early Christians have hacked out the sacred effigies, forgetting how

much of their own faith came straight from that which, to their heated imaginations, was peopled with devils and inspired by hell.

Rider seated against the background of the Egyptian monuments.
Cheyne Collection.

These kind of reflections had been preoccupying Rider ever since his first visit in 1887 when many of the tombs were being opened up and plundered for public display in Cairo. His dismay at the removal of the mummies from their ancient and sacred resting places was a symptom of his larger anxiety about what happened after death.

By March 5th they were back at the Mena House Hotel near the Pyramids and attempted to make travel arrangements for their return to England. Rider and Lilias were to lunch with some Egyptologists in Cairo. Rider comments, "I kept this [letter] open for Lilias to put in a line but she is too lazy. She sends her love." Was this an indication of Lilias' indifference to her mother or simply a holiday mood ?

From a letter dated March 8th, Rider reported that their travel negotiations continued. He and Lilias had been into Cairo for lunch with Mr Raphael and the Gardiners. "I came home [the Mena House Hotel] but Helen and Lilias went on to a tea party with Miss Lowther's friends. The Electric wire of the tram they returned in was broken but the Gippy driver charged at the gap. Result – the wire fell onto the tram vomiting blue flames – the Arab passengers bolted down the Embankment and its[sic] a mercy everybody was not electrocuted!

"They had to walk the rest of the way back. The incident is typical of this country now that its English managers are departing."[6]

Their arrangements complete at last, on Thursday March 13th Rider informed Louie (who was now in Paris) that they would be leaving for Port Said on the following Saturday, to pick up a boat on Monday 17th. They had not managed to get to Sakkara because of the strenuous journey and the cost.

By March 30th, Rider was back home in England and writing from St Leonard's-on-Sea and was very glad to be home. He had been to see Lord Curzon[7] to take

---

[6]   In February 1922 Britain unilaterally gave Egypt nominal independence but retained control over four key areas of government.

[7]   George Nathaniel Curzon, 1st Marquess Curzon of Kedleston, (1859–1925), who had been Viceroy of India and Foreign Secretary.

Rider in old age. Cheyne Collection.

him an Egyptian ring and he adds a postscript, "Wonder where Lilias and Helen slept last night. Their arrangements are extremely vague."

Lilias was part of a generation of women whose expectations of marriage had been severely thwarted by the devastating casualties of the First World War and this was particularly true of the upper classes: the fatalities amongst the officer class had been disproportionately high. It has been estimated that in the 1920s there were two million women "too many" and this social crisis was the subject of much hyperbolic publicity and discussion. No wonder then that not only Lilias and her cousin Joan, both in their early thirties, were unmarried, but also that Joan and Miss Samuel were openly man-hunting. Rider Haggard may have been perturbed by their antics but young women suddenly given the chance to meet new people on a trip such as this could not afford to lose any opportunity. Marriage was still the most socially approved state for women of all classes but particularly so for the upper echelons: they rarely had jobs or serious occupations (Joan eventually married an elderly widower, Sir George Buchanan, in 1930). On the other hand, times had changed radically as illustrated by fact that they could rush off to nightclubs as soon as they reached Cairo, something that would have been unheard just a few years previously. Lilias, although very sociable and entering into all the activities, was content with her father's company and a conventional life.

During 1924 Lilias took two more trips, probably visiting relatives and friends, but perhaps also keeping an eye out for suitors. It was quickly recognised that there were still opportunities for spinsters to find husbands abroad and in the colonies where the casualties had not been so devastating. The still wide circle of Haggard cousins stationed in various parts of the world served to facilitate this practice.

During 1924 Angie's husband Tom became ill with cancer and it was feared he would need a critical operation. After this last visit to Egypt Rider, reunited with his wife Louie, was well enough to honour some public engagements and to correspond with Rudyard Kipling. It is from this correspondence that Rider's disappointment at the end of his life is revealed. Over the winter of 1925 his health deteriorated again and he suffered months of pain and illness from a perforated ulcer and a bladder infection. His oldest friend from his Africa days, Arthur Cochrane, died in January 1925. In early February his youngest brother Arthur succumbed to a kidney disease. Soon afterwards William Carr, Rider's neighbour at Ditchingham Hall, also passed away. In the spring Rider underwent surgery in a London hospital for the ulcer; it was apparently successful but then swiftly and unexpectedly he developed another abscess. On May 14th he died.

For Louie and her two elder daughters his demise was the sad and momentous loss of an energetic and generous man of high achievement: a loyal husband and companion, a caring and beloved father. For Lilias, his death was on another scale entirely. It was seismic. The falling of a colossus. The breaching of a dam. It opened up an abyss, a chasm that could not be filled. Years later she recalled visiting the hospital room where his corpse lay ashen; his bony face still uncovered on the pillow, and recorded her reaction:

> Death was no stranger to her, but she stood for a moment filled
> with an unutterable dread. For the first time in her life, if she
> called there would be no answer, if she spoke no reply.[8]

The conversation of her life had suddenly stopped. There was not only no-one who could replace her father, but she had no other relationship with any comparable meaning. It is indicative of how significant her words were that they are almost identical to ones used by a psychotherapist of the late twentieth century, Maureen Murdock, who analysed women who identify with their father, said of her own father's death: "Without him there would be no one to hear me."[8]

Lilias may not have had any presentiment of the devastating effect Rider's death would have on her but it was abundantly clear to her observant friends and relatives. The letters of condolences sent to her refer again and again to her special relationship with Rider — some in terms that would seem more appropriate to a wife:

> I know you must feel his loss more than anyone as you and he
> were so devoted to each other.
>
> *Naomi Raikes, the Queen's Hotel, Toronto*

---

[8]   Maureen Murdock, *Fathers' Daughters: Breaking the Ties that Bind* (Louisiana: Spring Journal Books, 1994), 17.

to you especially the blow will be acute
Rev D.C. Tibbenham, 61 Wellesley Road, Great Yarmouth

I know too well the awful sorrow of losing one's father and yours
was more to you than most are — and we mourn
a very dear friend.
Susan M. Caletie, Langham Hotel, Portland Place, London W1

. . know what your father was to you and how much you loved
him.
Albertine Ross-Johnson, Mettingham Castle, Bungay

It must be a great comfort to feel what friends you and he were.
Margery [possibly Haggard]

An illustration on a book cover of Ayesha which was published in 1905.

But if the dialogue had stopped and the world gone silent, who exactly had Lilias been talking to? On one level her father was a delightful and amusing companion: a country gentleman who was also well-travelled and with a store of adventures behind him. What could be more natural than for a daughter to miss such a father? Yet, there was more to Rider than an agreeable and highly-coloured personality and when his spirit left his body about mid-day on May 14th 1925 it was more than just his personality that ceased to exist in this world. So too did Ayesha, the immortal goddess of his dreams. This goddess, whose haunting presence he had manifested in four of his wild tales of fiction, beginning with the best-selling *She* in 1887, *Ayesha* twenty years later in 1905, *She and Allan* in 1921, ending with *Wisdom's Daughter* in 1923, had a savage and relentless life of her own, and also a mesmeric beauty.

Lilias' conversation had been with a man possessed by a goddess. His complex psyche had given rise to some of the most startling novels of the High Victorian period. Freud is known to have had a dream about Haggard — an extraordinary convolution of relationship. However, it was Freud's one-time pupil Carl Jung who realised that Ayesha was more than the problem of one man and his *anima*, the feminine aspect of his soul: "She" was something to do with the collective unconscious and the psychological conundrums of the age. It was many years before this meaning was to be fully revealed through close reading of Rider's texts by Jung's pupil Cornelia Brunner.

What would have been very well known to Lilias was that at the dénouement of the novel *She*, before the protagonists Holly and Leo cross the abyss, the wind tore away Ayesha's cloak and "whirled it away into the darkness of the gulf".[9] When, a quarter of a century after Rider's death, Lilias wrote her biography of her father, she gave it the title *The Cloak That I Left* and cited for its origin a passage from the Bible — 2 Timothy, Chapter 4, 13:

> The cloke that I left at Troas with Carpus, when thou comest,
> bring with thee, and the books, but especially the parchments.

This quote gives Lilias a lovely resonance between her own writing — "especially the parchments" — and her father's. However, the "cloak" itself holds several meanings. It, too, can represent the "cloak" of writing, Rider's legacy, as well as the cloak of his identity and personality. But there was also this other cloak — Ayesha's cloak, floating freely out of space and time as Leo and Holly lie poised on a rocking stone above the abyss.

On that May morning in 1925 when Sir Henry Rider Haggard KBE the public figure, H. Rider Haggard the novelist and Rider Haggard the father and patriarch died, it was Lilias who faced an abyss. A cloak is a cover as well as a costume, it hides as well clothes. Ayesha's cloak is a cloak of the psyche. Lilias' cover was literally blown; she would have to face the world.

Murdock poses two alternatives: ". . . a father's daughter who embodies her father's unlived potential remains entrenched in hero worship and committed to long-term emulation of her father."[10] Or she might "grow beyond the psychology

9   *She* (London: OUP World's Classic, 1991, reissue 2008; first published 1887), 265.
10   Maureen Murdock, *Fathers' Daughters: Breaking the Ties that Bind* (Louisiana: Spring Journal Books, 1994), 71.

of a father's daughter to mould and craft the reality she wishes to bring into form." Murdock warns that "until she heals the deep wounding of her feminine nature, she will have no true power of her own." [11]

What had brought Lilias to that moment of unutterable dread? And what would life hold for her now?

---

[11]   Ibid, 99.

6

Off the Beaten Track

It is well-known that the successive deaths of male heirs during the First World War combined with the new tax of Death Duties decimated the inheritances of the land-owning classes. The historian of landscape, Peter Bishop, has noted that "In the ten years after the First World War, one quarter of English farming land changed hands."[1] There had not been such a large exchange since the Dissolution of the Monasteries. Amongst the new owners, many farms were bought on mortgages and, in the face of cheaper meat from abroad and low cereal prices at home, the farmers had trouble keeping up the payments. Making a living from farming had been precarious for decades. Rider, in his *War Diaries*, reckoned that if he took into account the lack of return on capital he had never made anything out of farming and had subsidised the Ditchingham estate by his writing; the estate had provided a hearth and home for his family and the experience for his agricultural books. He left four unpublished novels and his two-volume autobiography as legacies to his wife when he died.

The war had brought in its wake a social revolution on many levels: the class system, women's role in society and at home, living standards, diet, medicine, and industrial relations had all been changed or modified. In the years following the war there was a huge spurt of new house building both in the public sector with slums replaced by council flats and in the private sector with detached and semi-detached villas and bungalows. Much of this latter development was in the form of the suburb: ribbon developments stretching out in what were seen as octopus tentacles from an unruly urban body. The suburb, the site of conservative domestic dwellings, was anathema to "Preservationists" who wanted properly planned development to bring England into the modern world. They favoured the preservation of the urban and the rural as separate entities and saw suburbia as a direct threat to the old style English village or settlement;

---

[1]   Peter Bishop, *An Archetypal Constable* (London: Athlone, 1995), 116.

from this simple perception a whole moral and political stance was drawn.[2] Sir Patrick Abercrombie's book *The Preservation of Rural England* (1926) inspired the formation of the Campaign to Protect Rural England – the CPRE. Lilias was a founder member of the East Norfolk branch. She also took her place on the Ditchingham Parish Council and was an active member of the Women's Institute, the first branch of which had been founded in 1915 to encourage home-grown food and rural life. Lilias was establishing her areas of activity and influence.

Unemployment and strikes dogged Britain's recovery from the war. Mining areas were hardest hit but agriculture was not far behind.[3] In April 1923 there was a strike of agricultural workers in East Anglia. Rider and Louie were staying at St Leonard's-on-Sea but Lilias wrote to them from Ditchingham where she was spending Easter to say that not a man in their district was out on strike.[4] The dispute was settled by promise of a 25 shilling wage for a 50-hour week. The whole culture and fabric of rural life with all the skills that devolved on agriculture was in its death throes as urbanisation and suburbanisation drained it. The costs of wages for labour was still the major expense on farms where lack of capital made mechanisation slow. Susannah Wade Martins in *The Countryside of East Anglia: Changing Landscapes 1870–1950* argues that, contrary to contemporary perceptions, diversification of crops and government intervention did in fact help to alleviate the crisis.[5] The Land Settlement Act of 1919 was followed in 1926 by the Small-holdings and Allotments Act but farming had a lower return on capital than almost any other investment. An alternative model was envisaged through the Small Holdings Colonies Act which provided for the creation of farming co-operatives ("colonies") some of which still exist today. The Labour party took office for the first time in 1924 but fear of communism soon returned the Conservatives under Stanley Baldwin.

In this new, uncertain world, it was Lilias who began to take charge of life at Ditchingham. In terms of managing the now modestly-sized estate with the professional help of an agent it was a natural progression since Lilias had been closely involved and interested for many years and knew, from childhood, every field, lane, coppice and outbuilding. She also had the robustness for the work.

2   David Matless, *Landscape and Englishness* (London: Reaktion Books Ltd, 1998).
3   In November 1931 Clement Attlee said: "conditions in eastern England were
       indeed only comparable to those in some areas of abandoned mines or derelict
       towns'." Quoted in *The Agrarian History of England and Wales,* Volume 8 edited
       by Edith Whetham (Cambridge: CUP, 1967-2000), 237.
4   Rider Haggard's War Diaries April 2nd 1923, pages not numbered.
5   "Much of the impression of total depression which has passed into the
       folklore of farming was the creation of the contemporary farming press, and of
       polemicists like Henry Williamson and Adrian Bell, the latter keen to portray
       a decent way of life blighted by government inactivity and urban neglect"
       (Susannah Wade Martins).

After Tom Haggard died of cancer late in 1925, Angie had a nervous collapse and moved into the Gatehouse at the foot of the drive. Dolly and Colonel Cheyne, now retired from the army, with their three boys Archie (1911–1950), Reggie (1912–1962), and Mark (1917–2001) lived first at Kessingland Grange which was in a poor state since it had been requisitioned by the army during the war. After it was sold they moved into another family house, The Three Bells close to the Norwich-to-Bungay road. Lilias lived in Ditchingham House keeping her mother company while the Margitson cousins, the Turners, lived at Ditchingham Lodge (later Richard Haggard who had been shell-shocked lived there until his death in 1939); various other smaller houses and cottages on the estate were let. The family were all at home.

Then something less predictable happened.

Lilias persuaded her sister, aged forty-two, to adopt a baby girl whom they (or she) named Nada after Rider Haggard's heroine in his novel of Zulu romance *Nada the Lily*.[6] At the same time Lilias also persuaded her friend and cousin, Muriel Turner (née Harvey), whose daughter Georgina had died a few days after birth in 1913, to adopt a child, Joy, to become Nada's companion. This was a major intervention in the lives of a number of people.[7]

Nada was born in 1925 (coincidentally the year Rider died), arrived at Ditchingham at about nine months old in 1926 but was not formally adopted until November 1927. It was a private adoption and little is known about the circumstances. When she was about eight or nine years old Angie told Nada with great sensitivity that she was adopted and had been specially chosen. As a result Nada had no ill effects from the revelation although she did broach the subject with Lilias who told her that she had been chosen because she had a loud voice and a big nose like the Haggards. Later on Nada was told that she was the result of a liaison between a businessman and his secretary — both persons unknown to the family. Realising that chance had delivered her into fortunate circumstances she never pursued the matter further.

The sadly widowed Angie at last had a child to love but she was jealous of Lilias' interest in Nada and Nada, as she grew up, was aware that she must not show too much affection for Lilias — who now became "Aunt Lil". Nada was quite a timid child and did not always measure up to Lilias' standards of hardiness and, from the point of view of temperament, had a closer affinity to Angie. There was unease in the relationships and one wonders whether Lilias would have preferred, in more liberal times, to have adopted the child herself. Breeding in general was a country pursuit. Lilias kept bantams, bees, doves and ducks; she

---

[6]   Written in 1890 and published in 1892.
[7]   That Lilias initiated these adoptions is unsupported by documentary evidence but attested by her family.

Lilias with baby Nada and two dogs in the garden.
Cheyne Collection.

bred black rabbits (Blue Beverans), silkworms for the silk factory in Bungay, and canaries called Norfolk Rollers which she sold in Norwich and abroad. About this time she also started raising bull terriers with the specific objective of trying to breed more intelligent pedigree dogs; she showed them at Crufts.

The economic slide did not improve and in 1926 there was a General Strike of two and a half million workers but the populace turned out in sufficient number to "man" the essential services and the strike was defeated. Women over twenty-one were awarded the franchise in 1928 and the Labour Party was returned to office in 1929 — the year that saw the Wall Street financial crash. War debts and unemployment led to the Great Depression.

The British Empire Exhibition of 1924/5 at Wembley had been the largest exhibition held in the country since the Great Exhibition of 1851 but in reality the future of the Empire was proving much less certain than it had been before the War. In 1920 Ireland was partitioned, the following year the Government of India Act gave India some measures of self-government and, as has been noted, Egypt was given nominal independence. As the edges of the Empire started to unravel and the political ideals of the international Left began to spread, confidence in the identity of Great Britain was shaken; the definitions of what was abroad and what was home also became less clear cut. People were less and less sure what Englishness

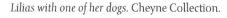

Lilias with one of her dogs. Cheyne Collection.

meant although they were still very sure that it was important.

One expression of this crisis was a quest for regional knowledge at home. Motor travel became more of a norm for the middle classes and H.V. Morton (1892-1979), a travel writer and journalist, led the way with explaining a conservative view:

> [it may be] difficult at first for the unaccustomed eyes of the townsman to understand that behind the beauty of the English country is an economic and a social cancer. An old order is being taxed out of existence; "our great industry" — as the experts call it — employs fewer men than those on the dole, and, struggling along, is facing insuperable difficulties with a blundering but historic stolidity. While our cornland (sic) is going back to grass year after year, our annual bill to the foreigner for imported foodstuffs is four hundred million pounds. Everywhere is the same story: mortgages on farms; no fluid capital; the breaking up of famous estates when owners die; the impossibility of growing corn because of the expense of labour and the danger of foreign competition; the folly of keeping cattle when the Roast beef of Old England comes so cheaply from the Argentine.[8]

After further discussion of the history and importance of villages, he concludes with a line that might well have been written half a century later with ecological and New Age concerns in mind:

> . . . and a streak of ancient wisdom warns us that it is our duty to keep an eye on the old thatch because we may have to go back there some day, if not for the sake of our bodies, perhaps for the sake of our souls.[9]

Lilias owned a succession of glamorous cars including an Hispano-Suiza — a make that was known for its luxury. Angie and Louie also had their own cars. The economy of the country and countryside might be on the slide but at Ditchingham in the late 1920s they still had two housemaids, a parlour maid (Gerty Perry), a cook and a kitchen maid. Outside there were three gardeners (the head gardener was Jimmy Perry, brother of Gerty), and a chauffeur called Mr Best for Lady Haggard. Some of the servants lived in cottages on Free Lane, many of which were owned by the estate. The agent was William C. Walker who lived at Pye's Hall, Wrentham. Lilias managed the smaller aspects of the estate and busied herself

8   H. V. Morton, *In Search of England* (London: Methuen, 1927), ix.
9   Ibid, xi.

Lilias on holiday by the sea — she often went on motor tours to Scotland and Wales. Cheyne Collection.

with the cottages and gardens. From the age of four Nada had a governess, a Miss Mabel Brown, whom she called Brownie. A Miss Peck, a dressmaker in the village, made some of Nada's clothes and perhaps some of the adults' as well. Miss Brown would also help with smocks and party dresses. Nada as she grew up had her own pony. Lilias would shop in London or in Norwich at the better dress shops.

Lilias knew everyone of any social standing in the county and had a particular circle of friends around the Ditchingham area: Kitty Athill from Ditchingham Hall,[10] the Meads at Earsham, the Crisps at Kirby Cane Hall, and Henta (Marie) Scudamore, widow of Hughie Scudamore whose father and grandfather had been vicars of Ditchingham over a period of sixty years. Lilias was distinctive with her golden corn-coloured hair now styled in plaits round her head, her almond eyes, her loud voice and long stride. She got on very well with men and animals and seems to have preferred dogs to human beings. She was known for the close, almost telepathic, communication she had with them. Unfortunately her bull terriers had a reputation for killing cats in the neighbourhood and the cats' skins would be put out to dry at the stables.[11]

Her nephew Adrian Webb, a regular visitor, respected her tremendously. Adrian's parents were Audrey (Jack and Aggie's youngest daughter) and Geoffrey Webb, a naval officer, who had been posted out to West Africa. In 1932 Audrey died of Blackwater Fever on a return voyage. Adrian thereafter stayed at Ditchingham every year; Lilias effectively gave him a second home. And she was, he said, always very kind and very sensible over family quarrels.

Lilias was not so good with young children. Nada remembered that her aunt could also be a terrible tease. She would hold up Nada's teddy bear to the bull terriers pretending that they would devour it. This upset Nada to the point of

[10]   Mother of Diana Athill, the editor and author.
[11]   Author's conversation with Margaret Ling, a niece of housemaid Gerty Perry, May 6th, 2009.

tears. Lilias would also be impatient of childish sensibilities telling Nada not to be a "fuss pot" or "not to be a prude" about changing for bathing in front of people.

Lilias was approaching her forties. In 1928 Lady Haggard bought her the Bath House, a two storey modest, but very interesting, property set in fourteen acres of land, which sat beside the Waveney marshes on the edge of the Ditchingham estate. It had once been part of a small eighteenth century spa complex where visitors came to take the waters from a lively mineral spring. The presence of the spring lent a spiritual quality to the property. The waters fed a "ram" which supplied the house but Lilias often struggled with the mechanism. She described the site herself:

> The valley here lies like a great saucer, and the river Waveney,
> leaving its direct course at Bungay, encircles the whole of Outney
> Common and marshes in a vast loop, returning to Bungay again,
> the town being built on higher ground in the neck of the loop.
> All around the valley are low hills, alternately wooded and rough
> pasture land. Shoot runs into shoot; Ellingham just beyond
> Bungay, then Ditchingham and Earsham on the loop, and
> beyond that the great expanse of the Flixton Woods, running up
> the river to Homersfield and beyond.[12]

The Bath House. Cheyne Collection.

[12]   *I Walked by Night.* ix.

It was a wonderful new challenge for Lilias' practical skills: she began renovating the dilapidated house with the help of local builders and craftsmen. It took some time to make it liveable and for many years she moved seasonally between Ditchingham House and the Bath House, letting the latter when it was eventually habitable to strangers. To her great joy she was able to create a new garden for herself. But if Lilias now had a home of her own it didn't make her any the less restless. She took many trips abroad, went up to London and to visit relatives on a regular basis. She loved the theatre and visiting historic houses and gardens and just getting out on the open road.

The way ahead was not clear; Rider's royalties would not last for ever and Lilias had ambitions that would not be satisfied by homemaking. In 1929 she enrolled in a correspondence course at the Premier School of Journalism, 45 Adam Street, Adelphi London WC2. Her father had encouraged her schoolgirl-interest in essays and plays: she decided to try her hand at writing.

The timing was excellent.

Newspaper editors were waking up to the fact that women were now a large part of their readership and they were looking for women journalists to supply features and commentaries. Moreover the subject of the countryside was taking new prominence.

H. J. Massingham, (1888–1952) also from Norfolk but based in London was treading a journalistic path through natural history and landscape; he was one of a group of writers known as "ruralists" along with Adrian Bell, a Suffolk farmer, A. G. Street, a Wiltshire farmer and author, Henry Williamson, a Devon-based author, and Crichton Porteous a prolific journalist from the Peak District. Massingham, who wrote for *The Field*, *The Spectator* and *Country Life*, was interested in Distributism, an ideology of property ownership that was an alternative to capitalism or communism, advocating a much wider spread of property ownership and more co-operative ownership that would subordinate economic activity to other more important human values. G. K. Chesterton and Hilaire Belloc (both Anglo-Catholics) were two of its strongest proponents[13] and the sources of this idea were in contemporary Roman Catholic social teaching, mixed with Cobbett and Ruskin.

In *The Genius of England* (1937) Massingham described the Isle of Axholme, north-west Lincolnshire, which had escaped the late Tudor Enclosures and "was still functioning as a small galaxy of village communities practising the open-field system".[14] Massingham quoted Rider's comment from *Rural England* to support his view: "One of the few places I have visited in England which is truly

13   *http://en.wikipedia.org/wiki/Distributism* – accessed 15/02/2014
14   H. J. Massingham *The Genius of England* (London: Chapman and Hall, 1937), 118.

prosperous in an agricultural sense." Massingham said of Haggard that he had "a passion for the restoration of English agriculture" which was a "guiding principle of a disinterested life."[15]

While Massingham and his *confrères* may have been naturalists and countrymen their books, stressing the anti-materialist values of country life and preaching a return to small farms, appealed to a readership that included liberal intellectuals intent on restoration rather than revolution who wanted to restore the status of yeomanry (of which more later) because they thought it would be a stabilising force against radicals.

There was an open gate for writing about country issues but at first Lilias wrote simply about historical subjects and travel articles. She was immediately quite successful in placing articles in the *Eastern Daily Press* and her first efforts were a series of six on the de la Pole family — a subject which she had mentioned in one of her letters from school. She followed with more history: the King's Lynn Treasure; Witchcraft; Tudor Norwich; the battle of Herrings — a story about Sir John Fastolf and herring barrels. In the summer of 1929 she wrote about Vesuvius and the Ruins of Pompeii (which she had presumably visited recently) and in September had a letter published in *Country Life* on Jack Russells and Bull Terriers. During the next few years she wrote a number of competent but not especially distinguished articles based on rural culture and history, the observation of animals, people she had known — for example a profile of Dr Ronald Ross — and some she had not: Joan of Arc and Christopher Wren ("A Tale of Old London"). She had the knack of using incidents and information from everyday life and turning them into an interesting read. Indeed she later described her method:

> I still "make pictures", a habit rudely referred to in the family
> circles as my "trances", adding to them odds and ends of
> information which fill in the landscape and lend substance
> and truth to their unsubstantial fabric . . . It makes possessions
> speak, the dry bones of history arise and walk, dead days come
> alive, and provides a way of escape from burdens . . .[16]

In 1929/30 Lilias wrote an introduction to a book by local author, Ethel Mann, who had been a friend of Rider's. *An Englishman at Home and Abroad: the diaries of J. B. Scott of Bungay 1792—1828.* It was an entirely parochial subject — a local philanthropist - but the title offers an interesting alignment with one of the preoccupations of the age: Englishness.

In 1932 Lilias moved into slightly deeper waters. Within a November article on

15   Ibid, 119.
16   *A Country Scrapbook,* 66.

food preservation, "The Progress of Canning", she mentioned the "Michaelmas forced sales" when the banks foreclosed on farmers so that farms worth £20 an acre changed hands for £4. Her comments were scarcely radical or inflammatory stuff.

It is not known exactly how and when Lilias met Margaret Spurrell but that they did meet is not at all surprising; they were both part of Norfolk county society and would have had many friends and relatives in common. Indeed Rider had been at Ipswich Grammar School with Robert and Edmund Spurrell who inherited Bessingham Manor in north Norfolk and they remained friends.[17] The Spurrells were an old Norfolk family that had farmed nearly a thousand acres at Thurgarton, north of Aylsham, for about 400 years. Margaret's father, John was the youngest son of Richard James Spurrell of Thurgarton Hall. John and his wife Violet lived first at Wiveton Hall and then at Weybourne on the north Norfolk coast. Margaret had an older half-brother John and a younger sister Phyllis. John died in August 1926, killed by a buffalo, out in Tanganika (now Tanzania) where he was working as an Administrative Officer.

By extraordinary good fortune and because he had once been land agent to the Countess of Rechberg, John inherited her estate of 2,700 acres at Horsham St Faiths just north of Norwich. It was there in the 1920s that he built a manor house for his family.[18] But Margaret's parents were not, apparently, well-matched. Her father is rumoured to have had two illegitimate daughters, to have kept a mistress in Norwich, and certainly to have fathered an illegitimate son in 1937.

Margaret Spurrell with two of her dogs.
Cheyne Collection.

Margaret, known to her friends as "Marg" was born in January 1904 in Sheringham, Norfolk and was twelve years younger than Lilias; she was dark-haired, very good looking in a bold way, very forthright and talented. She had independent means (possibly separate from her father's inheritance), had been a lady-in-waiting to a Lord Mayor of London, had a flat in Mayfair and both she and her younger sister Phyllis drove sports cars. She was tremendously sociable and rather dashing. She followed the usual country pursuits – gardening, shooting and bird watching – with

17   Jonathan C. Spurrell, *Rider Haggard Society Journal*, No 98, September 2010.
18   Julian Eve, *The Story of a Village: a Vistory of Horsham St Faith* (Norwich: 1992).

enthusiasm. Both she and her sister learned to fly and were members of the Norfolk and Norwich Aero Club. Later she sketched and painted, reportedly quite competently.[19]

Margaret and Lilias became close friends and, whether they were aware of it or not at this stage, they had found in each other a life partner.

Then Lilias had another piece of luck. Mrs Longrigg, wife of John Longrigg the farm manager, showed her a notebook of memories written by an old Norfolk character. The author was well-known to Lilias:

> For many years he had been something of a local celebrity, and
> had appeared with great regularity before my father on two local
> Benches. The sound of his gun was also familiar in our ears.[20]

The character's name was Frederick Rolfe. He styled himself "King of the Norfolk Poachers" and he hailed from Pentney, not far from West Bradenham. In his later years he ended up in Bungay, in a number of different domiciles, and at one point in an isolated hut on the edge of the Ditchingham estate where he started writing up notes about his life. If Rolfe was not unknown to Lilias, then neither were poachers as a breed, but to her readers he was a rare and intriguing character. She first introduced him through two articles, April 1st and April 8th 1933, in *Country Life*, the monthly magazine for the landed classes and for those who aspired to their tastes. The first one had the title "The Life and History of the King of the Norfolk Poachers — Written by Himself" . "We are indebted for this remarkable narrative to Miss Lilias Rider Haggard who transcribed the original manuscript and vouches for its authenticity."

The two articles had no introduction or context and were simply Rolfe's own story but much abbreviated in comparison with what was to follow. Evidently the articles were appreciated; Lilias realised that she had hit a rich vein of interest. She decided to produce a book but to do so would need a good deal more information from Rolfe and a wider context for her readers.

There was a tradition for this kind of subject: Richard Jeffries' *The Amateur Poacher* (1879); *The Gamekeeper at Home* (1878); George Bourne's *Talks with a Surrey Peasant* (1901) and W. H. Hudson's *A Shepherd's Life* (1905). However, Norfolk was still a very isolated area, unknown and undiscovered and difficult to discover because of its remoteness and because so much of it was privately owned agricultural land. Above all Norfolk people prided themselves on their isolation and indifference to the rest of England; they were suspicious by nature,

---

[19]　Information from author's interviews with Marie Wilcox 30/01/08, Mrs R Winch spring 2007, Rosamund Woodton 29/10/08, and Richard Spurrell 16/01/2007.

[20]　*I Walked By Night*, v.

spoke a heavy dialect and were not interested in explaining themselves. In the 1930s when people were becoming more acutely aware that the mechanisation of agriculture was killing rural life there was a curiosity and appetite for what was obviously not going to survive another generation. Rural culture was slipping through the sieve of historical record because the tradition was oral — so many country people having been illiterate. But Frederick Rolfe was not illiterate and he had found, either by chance or design, a mediator.

Rolfe's memoirs were not spontaneous. In her introduction Lilias wrote:

> It is entirely his own work, but it was not written as it appears
> here, as it was in no way consecutive. It came to me in letters
> and scraps of paper, in old exercise books, on anything that
> was at hand when answering some random question of mine.
> Sometimes, like a water-diviner, I hit the spring and the twig
> twitched; at others it was a case of "no contact".[21]

> I have done but little pruning; most of my work has been
> arrangement of material so as to make the book a narrative, with
> the incidents in their right places. Also such minor services to
> the MS. as punctuation and some revision of spelling, although
> much has been left exactly as he wrote it. The Ballads are largely
> his.[22]

The book which was born of this co-operation is not simply a text but an artefact which was potentially desirable on many levels. Lilias developed the style of H. V. Morton which included layers of information in different formats: text interleaved with ballads and rhymes from a variety of sources and country lore. Footnotes giving lengthy additions and information added to its interest and plausibility and, with a masterstroke, Lilias commissioned illustrations from her friend Ted (Edward) Seago, a talented Norfolk artist with a rising reputation. Some of these are very particular to the story and landscape and some are more general but they endow the book with a style and atmosphere.[23] Most particularly they emphasize the poverty of dress and circumstances, the closeness to animals, the metaphor of the patient heavy horses and the timelessness of agricultural landscape. Lilias wrote a dedication of thanks to those who helped with the book:

> It is a matter of some satisfaction to me that this book is a local
> product. The Author, Editor, and Illustrator live within a radius
> of seven miles.[24]

[21]   *I Walked by Night*, vi.
[22]   Ibid, vi and vii.
[23]   The whereabouts of the original illustrations is unknown.
[24]   At this time Seago lived at the village of Brooke, a few miles north of
       Ditchingham.

The book, called *I Walked by Night: Being the Philosophy of the King of the Norfolk Poachers, Written by Himself*, was first published in 1935 by Nicholson & Watson and cost 15 shillings. It was widely reviewed in the national and regional

The front cover of the third edition of I Walked by Night

papers and the Book Society recommended it. A feature in the *Eastern Daily Press* was called "Excise [sic] Book Discovery" and the paper also reviewed it as an autobiography on October 4th 1935 but without any attempt at literary criticism. A year later it was published in the United States by E.P. Dutton. There is no doubt that the book made a mark.

Despite Lilias' protestations that the book was entirely Rolfe's work she did credit herself with the role of editor:

> I have let some paragraphs in the book stand which might, for
> various reasons, have been cut. My object was that those who
> read it might see the writer as he is (not as I might romantically
> have imagined him), with all his obvious crudities of opinion
> and strange code of honour.[25]

In fact it was a tremendously romantic book both from its theme of a lost country world of the 1870s and 1880s and from the particular story of Frederick Rolfe.

Lilias added another validation:

> You must have lived long among the people of East Anglia to
> understand at all some of his points of view. They are a strange
> people "born of the East Wind", as my father used to tell me:
> intensely suspicious of strangers (you remain one for at least
> thirty years after arrival in these parts), and often possessing a
> curious twist of mind.[26]

She then gave the reader her credo — a guide to how they were to receive this material:

> I hold no brief for a stagnant world. I have seen too much
> of the bitter fruit of ignorance and apathy in country places.
> "Enlightenment", as our author has it, must come, and its
> banners go before in the shape of advertisement hoardings and
> cheap literature.[27]

While dissociating this book from "cheap literature" she appeared to make clear that she was not looking to return to the old days except to enjoy a little armchair nostalgia:

> There is, however, a breadth, a simplicity and an unhurried
> dignity about life in these remote villages, which are even yet
> untouched by the motor bus, the cinema, and the summer
> visitor. [28]

[25]   *I Walked by Night* vii.
[26]   Ibid,vii.
[27]   Ibid, x.
[28]   Ibid, x.

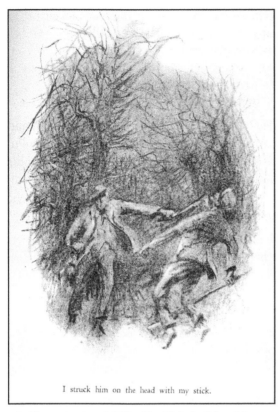

I struck him on the head with my stick.

An illustration from I Walked by Night *by Edward Seago.*

The evocation of the past can be powerful critique of the present. It would seem that she was having her cake and eating it too — and allowing her readers the same indulgence.

In the introduction Lilias sets up Rolfe's validity as a countryman by the story of how he could "charm" warts from the Longriggs' son. This was a vanishing practice from days before any formalised medicine and encompasses the idea that science isn't the only way to understand the world.

The narrative of the book follows the hero through his impoverished country childhood in rural west Norfolk to a life of restless troublemaking and poaching. By his own admission he was a tear-away and he recounted stories of his rebellion that led to exclusion from school and episodes of mischief in the village. The friction between him and his stepfather, who was dogmatically religious and in awe of his masters, exacerbated the young Rolfe's waywardness and stubbornness. His mother was not nearly so rigid but she was ruled by her husband. Rolfe found sympathy with his maternal grandparents who were easy-going and amicable; an uncle had been deported for sheep stealing and made good in Australia. Forbidden to visit them, he continued to see them secretly and thus early learned to deceive. It was in his early boyhood, too, that he learned to catch rabbit and later to poach pheasant and hare. He soon found that the excitement of poaching suited his temperament and it was a preferable occupation to the excruciatingly poorly-paid farm-labouring (all quotes from *I Walked by Night* are just as written in the text, keeping the flavour of the vernacular speech and spelling) :

> The Children was sent out at an early age into the fields to work, scaren crows and such like Jobs. I can well rember wen lots of

> poor Children had to go to work in the Spring of the year, picken
> foule grass, and other Jobs, from eight in the morning till five
> in the afternoon, some with scarse any boots on there feet. The
> Master would send a man to keep them at work, and he would
> stand in the field with a stick or whip to keep them at it. Wen they
> had done the day's work they would get the sum of three Pence.[29]

At a young age he was arrested and thrown into Norwich Castle prison and
had to face the horrors of the treadmill[30] and near starvation. This dreadful
experience was countered by a love match with a young woman who shared his
nocturnal adventures and had her own way with animals. He had met his soul
mate and they lived together for about four years but the idyll was to have a tragic
end when she died giving birth to a baby boy.

> I had to go on liven with out her, and could scarcely beleve it at
> first. I missed her so for many a year, and many a night wen I
> have been out on the Job, I have laid quiet behind a hedge wen
> the dogs have been worken a field, and fancied I have herd her
> laugh beside me, and say — "Here they come" as she used to do.[31]

Careless of his own safety, he once more got in trouble with the law and to
avoid prosecution fled from Norfolk to the anonymity of Manchester under a
false name. His descriptions of working class industrial Manchester and the
sporting life he enjoyed there provide a salty contrast to Norfolk. After six years
and having found a new wife, Rolfe received a letter from his old mother asking
him to come back since his father was dying. So he returned to rural life, facing
up to a spell in prison, and eventually a more settled time with two more children.
He was continually up before the Bench but was usually able to pay the fines. In
his middle years he even worked as a gamekeeper in the Waveney Valley. Towards
the end of the First World War (which claimed his first born son) he joined up
and became regimental rat-catcher at Bawdsey on the east Suffolk coast and thus
for the first time he enjoyed several years of regular wages before returning to his
old poaching ways, this time in the Bungay area.

Rolfe's life story is threaded through with accounts of country customs but
despite this appealing picturesqueness Rolfe returns repeatedly to the harshness
of agricultural life and the unfairness of the legal and social rules on the poor
labourers who were the foundation of the whole system. He equated the curse of
tilling the soil with the mark of Cain:

---

[29]   Ibid, 88.
[30]   The civil engineer Sir William Cubitt of Buxton, Norfolk invented the treadmill
         for prisoners early in the nineteenth century.
[31]   *I Walked by Night* 60.

All and everyone is dependent upon the tiller of the Soil. He is
the Father of all Workers, like the old saying has it:

The King he governs all
The Parson pray for all,
The Lawer plead for all,
The Ploughman pay for all
And feed all.
The Land is the Mother of all from beginning to end — as was
promised — from dust thou came and to dust thou shalt return.[32]

By some means or another Rolfe has grasped the thoughts of his fellow East
Anglian, Thomas Paine, and although no supporter of the church or religion
he had also thought about the teaching of the Bible.[33] Somewhere under all his
ruminating on the dreadful conditions of the past and cruelty to children, what
he is talking about is equality, and how we fail to manifest it in society and how
people manage somehow to live as best they can without it. And if that means law-
breaking, then so be it. He was willing to pay the price and he was unrepentant.

The strong character that comes through the book is one of a man who
can look after himself and, more
importantly for the potential reader of
this book, think for himself. He is no
mindless peasant. He is independent
of the system. For the urban reader
this does not put him into what they
would consider the criminal classes.
His thieving is of a kind that does not
impinge on their moral claims at all.
The pheasants and hares might, after
all, belong to anyone. It is the law of
capital that says they belong to the
landowner.

There is also a much older model
for this kind of law-breaking: it is
Robin Hood and the Greenwood
and taking the King's deer. If you are
hungry, is it wrong to feed yourself
or your family from what used to be
common land, common forests? This

Frederick Rolfe — King of the Norfolk Poachers.
Cheyne Collection.

[32]   Ibid, 103.
[33]   Ibid, 61.

is an appeal to Old England.

According to Lilias herself, many people questioned whether the book was "true". She made a defence of literary integrity and of the advisability of honesty in any business venture.

> The public, contrary to general belief, is extremely difficult to hoodwink. Invariably some enquiring mind checks a statement, and, filled with righteous joy at discovering an error, post-haste puts pen to paper in order to reveal it in all its horrid nakedness.[34]

So it seems undoubtedly "true" that these memories were presented to Lilias by Rolfe. The first two notebooks are in Bungay Museum. However, Charlotte Paton came up with a rather different story in her 2009 biography *The King of the Norfolk Poachers*. According to her research Rolfe had been twenty years old when he first went to prison, not a young lad; his wife Anna Carter had not been an orphan and had not been in service, she had been living with family members, nor did she die in childbirth; Rolfe deserted her when he went on the run to Manchester. They already had a three year old boy, young Fred, but the child born at that time was a girl not a boy and she died aged eight months. His wife didn't die until 1888 in Ditchingham after which he came back to Norfolk with his new wife Kitty. They had two children, Emily and Joubert. There is a period between 1903 and 1916 when Paton found it impossible to trace his activities. Young Fred never went to the battlefields of France but died aged 32 in Downham Market workhouse. Rolfe either had a poor memory or was a storyteller *par excellence*: the love story and loss of his soul mate is a very seductive element in the book.

Lilias gave validity to a story she had not verified – probably could not easily verify in those days before county record offices and microfilmed records.[35] A man who can call himself "King of the Norfolk Poachers" is a natural self-publicist – presumably for the public house audience. He was no fool and perhaps when he left the first notebook with Mrs Longrigg he was already thinking how to catch his pheasant.

Lilias paid him an initial £20 [equivalent to approximately £1200 in today's currency]. There is also a note of a payment of £7 10s signed by Rolfe and a separate note from Lilias that he was also paid half the royalties from her publisher through Barclays Bank: a substantial bag for the old poacher.

---

[34]   LRH, *A Country Scrapbook*, 47.
[35]   It is worth recalling Rider's ruse in creating, with Agnes Barber, a mock-up of the sherd of Amenerteas covered in heiroglyphs for the launch of *She*. It is still in a drawer in Norwich Castle Museum.

7

Cross Country

With the success of *I Walked by Night* Lilias was offered a weekly diary column for the *Eastern Daily Press* under the title and by-line "The Country Woman's Week".[1] It was published initially on the women's page on Mondays, starting on March 30th 1936, and related to the days of the previous week: the first days of spring. It began as if in mid-stream of a companionable narrative (the grammar is as in the original newspaper text):

> Sunday, March 22.
>
> A lovely warm day and we went for a picnic down to the cottage [the Bath House]. I took the punt over the river to the common [Bungay Common] to see if I could find any trace of the mixed seeds I had sown over the mud banks left by the dredger. All last summer the cattle and horses delighted in dragging up any brave plants which struggled to grow in the slimy mass. Fifty irises which I had divided with an aching back and ferried over to adorn the view, went in a single night, just pulled up, chewed and spat forth in disgust. Even rabbits will only eat irises when hard pressed. I was cheered to find quite a lot of seedlings had survived: Alyssum, snow in summer, aubrietia, pansys [sic] common saxifrage. Oriental and Shirley poppy, cornflower, larkspur, and several more not yet distinguishable. I fear the first week in May when the stock [cattle] come on will see the end of them. Protected the great expanse of mud would have been a riot of colour, which proved flowers will grow on newly dredged mud.
>
> The swans are thinking of housekeeping and getting very cross. They hiss and ruffle up every time the dogs run down the bank.

[1]   In the same newspaper there was a report of Hitler gaining a legal mandate by an election vote of nearly one hundred per cent.

Monday, 23rd.

Old G [Gorbell] finished putting in the briar roses in the wild bit
at the cottage. I have wired all this piece — an effort to defeat the
rabbits. Two weeks trapping early in the month accounted for
three hundred, but there seems no difference in their numbers!

. . .

Tuesday, 24th.

Three days of spring have worked a miracle. A week ago the
countryside was burnt and seared with frost and snow, nothing
had moved. To-day the bronze of the beach buds is washed
with silver and the elm tops thick with madder flowers. Down
in the wood by the river a faint veil of green spreads over the
dead leaves underfoot, the dog's mercury[2] thrusting up its little
spears. Above the marsh three couple of snipe mount and plane
in a frenzy of spring fever, the curious and unexplained bleating
drum of their downward swoop filling the air. Over the common,
the sandpipers are calling, passing spring visitors these — like
the seven Canadian geese who came last spring from some North
Norfolk preserve.

. . .

Wednesday, 25th

A creeping fog has swept over the countryside borne in from the
sea by a faint but icy north-east wind. Spring is lost — muffled in
a shroud and the hyacinths by the cottage garden path look as
if they blossomed untimely in November. The ewes and lambs
have all been moved up from the lambing pens to the meadows
near the house and all day and night their plaintive cry echoes
through the fog. Few animals can sound so desolate.
    Last night the thin sickle of the new moon lay on her back
bearing the ghostly body of the old moon in her arms. She came
in perfect weather early Monday but they say here a moon early
seen seldom seen. N. [Nada] and I duly bowed three times and
wished!

. . .

2   Mercurialis perennis.

Thursday, 28th.

Another foggy, raw day. A very indignant gardener took me
down the kitchen garden this morning to see the wreck of his
seed beds. Arriving early he found fourteen pheasants and about
twenty jackdaws raiding his peas and beans, which they were
digging out from under the wire guards.

. . .

Friday, 27th.

A Parish Council meeting, a body on which I sit a lone female
with eleven good men and true. The chief business was the
retirement of our sexton after many years' service but, as he said
to me "When old age comes there isn't no escape," and grave
digging is heavy work. He asked me if I would take his last lot of
"stones" off him. The cemetery was placed by the "the powers
that were" a generation back on the site of the best ice-borne
gravel deposit for miles around! My father used to say that owing
to the rare preservative qualities of gravel everyone would come
out 1000 years hence as fresh as they went in, and, to judge
from a certain prehistoric gentleman from gravel deposits in the
British Museum, it seems likely.

. . .

Saturday, 28th.

Planted two dozen Regale and Henry lilies under the rosemary
hedge. Put in deep, with pockets of sand round them they will,
I hope, do as the soil is light loam, and neither lily is intolerant
of lime in moderate quantities. Both reach six or seven feet, and
extraordinarily lovely when in blossom.

Lilias had begun on a steady journalistic career and through the columns
established a presence throughout the eastern counties. She wove the daily
happenings of her life and her family with threads of history, folk-lore, country
crafts and skills, recipes, scraps of poetry, local traditions and musings on nature
and life. The style was gentle but straightforward, similar to her father's narrative
in *The Gardener's Year*: highly observant of nature and farming together with wry
comments on the daily round and frustrations of life. To this she gradually slipped
in occasional, almost Wodehousean, humour. While she could be sentimental

The Bath House with its surrounding gardens planted by Lilias.
Cheyne Collection.

about patriotism, religion and royalty she was quite brisk about country life. It
was a perfect combination of a depth of knowledge of nature with an underlying
presumption of conservative values with which so many of her readers could
identify. She included a cast of characters: Gorbell the gardener, George Baldry
the builder and hirer-out of boats, her friends Ted Seago, Kitty Athill, Henta
Scudamore, her family and, of course, Margaret. In the beginning she used only
initials for their names but as she grew more confident she relaxed this.

The topics she discussed and described were wide-ranging although in the
early days she stuck close to gardening and landscape; like any new columnist she
was finding her feet. That spring of 1936 she let out the Bath House and rented
a tiny cottage in the picturesque old fishing village of Blakeney, opposite the
White Horse public house. Blakeney had a "huddle of red-roofed cobble houses",
"old granaries and boat sheds", "courts, alleyways and flint-walled gardens". Her
small double-doored cottage was so small that, as she described it in her column,
"downstairs I have my feet in the street, so to speak, and upstairs my head in
my opposite neighbour's windows. However, two paces out of the front door lies
a view even more boundless than at home . . ." The cottage shared a well in a
courtyard with its neighbours and bathing was undertaken in a large tin saucer
with water heated in a copper and tea towels draped over the windows for privacy.
It was the beginning of many years of happy summers on the North Norfolk coast
for all her family, especially Nada and many of Lilias' nephews and nieces. They

The 'Double-door' cottage in Blakeney with members of the Haggard family outside the door.
Cheyne Collection.

could spend the days out on the marshes bird-watching or sailing out around the Point to see the seals and wider vistas of the classic Norfolk coastal landscape.

While organising the move Lilias stopped to watch some aeroplanes of a "circus" practising their formations and wondered how long it would be before the hum of aeroplanes became part of their daily lives, although at this time she seems to be thinking not of war but of increasing mechanisation and its deleterious effects on civilisation. In newspapers and magazines the threat of Hitler's brand of Fascism was not yet realised; the Spanish Civil War did not begin until later in the year. An article in March 28th edition of *Country Life* featured "Hitler as a Countryman", subtitled "The 'Squire' of Wachenfeld'" written by "Ignatius Phayre".[3] "Phayre" wrote pieces for other UK magazines representing Hitler in domestic settings. The significance of them is in a propagandist writer trying to insinuate Hitler into the strands of life that were still the preoccupations of English culture — the making of houses and gardens, village life, old country ways.

It was to these preoccupations that Lilias responded so well with her easy contact with the old countrymen and women of the district who still worked in the old ways. Of Baldry she wrote:

> To-day Baldry put the finishing touches painting the stable and cow-house. After sixteen months this great work is finished. It consists of a large loose-box, a calf box, two cow stalls, a

[3]   The pen name of an Irish writer called William George Fitzgerald.

dairy with sink and tap, and upstairs three good rooms, with
dormer windows, connected by sliding doors. Water is laid on
to dairy and cow stalls, a soft water tank provided in addition,
and all done in accordance with the latest ideas. Baldry has
built it entirely single-handed with a little labouring help from
his brother, and no new thing has been used except the steel
windows and stall fittings, about half the bricks and some
planking for floors etc. He even made the rollers and tracks for
the doors from some of his "scraps", and was really distressed
because he could not "find up" a couple of taps needed, and had
to buy them. The infinite patience and careful workmanship
given to the whole job, and physical endurance brought to it (for
Baldry is over seventy), has kept me in constant admiration. In
addition the building from my design and his adaption is by no
means ugly and quite in keeping with the house.[4]

Rudyard Kipling had died in January and, when his will was published, Lilias
noted that he had left a bequest to the Fairbridge Farm Schools which were
dedicated to settling orphaned or deprived children on farms in the colonies.
The organisation's aims were very much in line with pre-World War I ideas about
child migration to "empty" lands of South Africa, Australia and Canada. Probably
following Rider's lead, Lilias herself supported them for she wrote:

The same day I received their report of the work done in the
distressed areas — a heart-breaking document. Many of us will
remember how the men in hospital during the war of 1914–18
used to sing with such enthusiasm:

There's a good time coming, a'coming and a'humming,
There's a good time coming for us all.

In the bitter years since the war they have come to full knowledge
of that "good time" and have seen their children inherit, not
a brave new world, but misery, poverty, and squalor, and have
been powerless to help them. The Fairbridge Farm Schools are a
creative effort in the general negation, the try to do, while most
intellectuals merely criticise and talk, and do — nothing.[5]

Lilias followed her own advice and took an active interest in helping some of
the pupils; a boy called Abbot Smith from the Rhodesian Fairbridge farm school
came to stay with her and married his fiancée, also a Fairbridge pupil, from the

4   LRH Norfolk Life, 29
5   Ibid, 19.

Bath House. They became personal friends. However, there was a darker side to the Schools, as there was to Barnardo and Catholic settlement schools, which only came to light many decades later. Not all the children were orphans or willing immigrants, especially to Australia and Canada. Poverty drove parents to send their children away and, without any communication or avenue of appeal, cruelty and abuse could and often did flourish. In the 1930s attitudes to family, child care and social work were changing in the light of the new science of psychology but the farm schools were still part of the old ideas of "saving children from what was seen as circumstances of moral and material deprivation".[6]

In June Lilias took a trip to London and went to see Eric Portman in *Bitter Harvest* about the life of Lord Byron and soon after joined a Haggard family fishing holiday in Wales. Driving across country alerted her to the fact that few places "allow their inhabitants to deface the villages with hideous wall and post advertisements to the same degree as they do in the Eastern Counties".[7]

On her return she went up to the coast, although perhaps only for weekends, in the early part of the summer. Her fame was growing and she wrote with self-deprecating humour about its effect:

> . . . felt much flattered at getting a letter asking me to join a
> lecture association. Here was someone appreciating me at my
> true worth thought I, especially when I observed canons, deans,
> and even a bishop figured amongst my co-lecturers. There was
> only one other woman, a lady whom I have met and who is a
> great authority on Egyptology. Doubt seized me when I read
> the lectures were intended to entertain, instruct, and uplift the
> audience. Then I saw that bees was to be the suggested subject of
> my first effort. Bees! Most certainly I could give a lecture on bees,
> a most graphic account of my sufferings and complete defeat at
> their hands or rather tails. But would it either uplift or instruct?
> My little black old English bees, holding up motor-cars, expert
> in instant injection of formic acid to check one's benevolent and
> orderly plans for their regularisation! I could perhaps entertain,
> but only the bees themselves could achieve the uplift! [8]

In July she listened to the broadcast of the unveiling by the King of the Canadian Memorial at Vimy Ridge which she herself had visited in October 1925. Her preferred epitaph consisted of lines from Swinburne's poem *Dolores*. Algernon

[6]   Geoffrey Sherington and Chris Jeffrey, Chris, *Fairbridge: Empire and Child Migration* (London: Woburn Press, 1998), 187.
[7]   *Norfolk Life*, 45.
[8]   Ibid, 55.

Swinburne was a highly sensual late-Victorian poet whom she mentions several times over the years as a favourite.[9] The summer of 1936 was unrelentingly wet but she spent the August Bank Holiday on the coast bird-watching – probably with Margaret.

Her two bull terriers slept on her bed (she wore a lace night cap) and she interpreted their barking into human language.[10] A new bloodhound joined the family in August much to Nada's delight, and Lilias thought he would have

Lilias in summer with one of her bull terriers.
Cheyne Collection.

a calming effect on her terriers but unfortunately this was not the case. The rain continued causing misery to the chickens and the farmers. As autumn approached farm-sale fixtures began to appear in the local papers. Lilias reviewed the situation at Ditchingham,

Turning up our sale catalogue when the farm was handed over to a tenant in 1917 made me realise the drop in agricultural values. The live and dead stock on about four hundred acres fetched £7,615. Seven years later its equivalent value was probably about £3,000 or less.[11]

What Lilias did not allude to was the farmers' growing antagonism to paying the church tithes and the war that wasbeing waged against this ancient tax just down the Waveney Valley at a farm in Wortham. Doreen Wallace's *The Tithe War* had been published in 1934 bringing to public attention the impossibility of making ends meet under current circumstances. When farmers refused to pay the tithe the county courts initiated forced Distraint Sales of their live and dead stock. This led to public demonstrations, boycotting of church services and

9   An article by Clara Watts-Dunton about Swinburne's visit to Poppyland had
        appeared in the July 25th 1936 edition of *Country Life*. On the centenary of
        his birth in 1937 Lilias wrote an appreciation of his craftsmanship and of the
        coastal scenes he evoked; Swinburne "knew well the long stretch of coast from
        Cromer to Wells". (*Norfolk Life*, 147), which points to Lilias being a regular
        reader of the magazine.
10   *Norfolk Life*, 63.
11   Ibid, 67.

a variety of "tricks" on both sides. Amongst the supporters of the hard-pressed farmers were contingents of Moseley's followers who created a dramatic sight in the fields, the colour of their shirts against the corn and fears about their politics giving rise to the gathering-in being called the Black Harvest.

The autumn weather improved and the Haggards and Cheynes continued to go up to Blakeney and out to the Point while the swallows gathered. The Reverend John Scudamore, for so long vicar of Ditchingham, died. A ship, a Dutch motor vessel, the *Karazan*, was grounded on the shingle and while this drama unfolded Lilias described thatching techniques and a trip to Holkham. Then restless as ever Lilias went off on a trip through Germany. From the Hook of Holland she and Margaret motored down to Munich, Köln, Bonn, Koblenz and Frankfurt. They then moved up into the mountains of Bavaria where dreadful weather threatened the migrating birds, which caused Lilias considerable anxiety and concern. So severe was their plight that the birds were being collected up in crates and flown south to Venice. Lilias' choice of reading to inform herself about Germany was *The Ludwigs of Bavaria* by Henry Channon. Wildlife continued to take her interest before a final expedition to Oberammergau coming back via Munich. She made no mention in her travel articles of what, by late 1936, must have been fairly obvious — the pervasive presence of the Nazis — but later in *A Country Scrapbook* she notes that where she would have expected to see country people wearing traditional costume she saw only uniforms.[12] Either the *Eastern Daily Press*, or she, did not wish to include this kind of observation.

On her return Lilias resumed her weekly journal with accounts of apple picking, chicken breeding and the campaigns of the Council for the Preservation of Rural England to protect the landscape. When it came to the felling of trees Lilias had deep resistance and recalled another favourite author, Charlotte Mew, whose poem The Trees are Down starts with the line: "Half the spring for me will have gone with them" and ends, "But I, all day, I heard an angel crying; 'Hurt not the trees.'"[13] Lilias' daily round on the estate involved inspecting farm buildings and cottages, estimating and organising repairs and reconstructions but she was relieved that her responsibilities did not include "the anxieties of farming" too. "The land is a hard taskmaster . . . and it becomes a load only the toughest men can endure."[14] With this in mind she felt nothing but amusement for Polish author Rom Landau's ideals in his book *Seven* about every citizen working the land for several months a year in order to stay in touch with the laws of nature.[15]

12 *A Country Scrapbook*, 88.
13 Charlotte Mew (1869– 1928) a poet, much admired by Thomas Hardy, who published her first collection of poetry *A Farmer's Bride* in 1916.
14 *Norfolk Life*, 99.
15 Rom Landau (1899–1974), author, reviewer, journalist and educator.

Lilias with her new cider press — the start of a hobby she wrote about in her columns. Cheyne Collection.

She thought there was precious little inspiration to be drawn from lifting sugar beet in the driving rain. It was this humour and realism that separated her from other, politicised, country writers of the period.

She had less detachment about the abdication on December 11th 1936 of the new King Edward VIII. She wrote with theatrical sense of tragedy that "The integrity of the Crown has demanded of the country a terrific sacrifice." And "The whole nation mourns the bitter necessity of what goes forward in the Houses of Parliament."[16]

In her October 5th column she reflected on the summer idyll:

> Gone into the limbo of memory are the long lazy mornings drifting with idle sail on a mirrored sea, the shore hazed in mist like the bloom on a plum. The picnic lunches on the Point, the sand hot between bare toes, watching the gannets diving like plummets after herring, and round-headed, mild-eyed seals slip out of the waves and lollop awkwardly on to the sloping beach. The golden evenings down on the muds, full of the sound of sea birds' wings, and the sad, empty notes of their calling — the very voice and spirit of the marshes. Gone until "next year", which always seemed such an infinity in childhood.

This area of Norfolk was very familiar to Margaret, who had been born at Wiveton Hall, just east of Blakeney. She was also a keen bird-watcher and had a caravan positioned for the purpose on mudflats along a creek called the Morston Freshes to the west of Blakeney.

Over the Christmas holiday Lilias read the newly published *Honourable Estate*, a novel by Vera Brittain about different kinds of marital partnerships before and during the first World War.[17] Lilias noted:

Margaret outside her caravan. Cheyne Collection.

> I was left speculating if any women could in reality have borne up against the successive miseries endured by the principal [fictional] characters and retained their sanity, much less their working efficiency. The world is

---

[16]   LRH, *Norfolk Life*, 107.

[17]   Vera Brittain (1893–1970) author of *Testament of Youth*, a feminist and pacifist.

a hard road to those who feel acutely, and the books of many
writers bear the stamp of the generation who bore the full
burden of the war. Bitterness against their lot has entered into
their souls. They are in chronic revolt against the circumstances
of an era which destroyed the lovely beginnings of their lives, and
left them desolate. Their literature, though vivid, is bitter.[18]

Lilias seemed to consciously avoid that bitterness in her writings and always
took heart from what she could find in her surroundings and her family. Her
application to the practical problems of the land ensured her sanity:

My great problem at the Cottage is shelter from the east, for there
I am unprotected, and the pitiless bite of a wind-frost spreads
havoc and desolation to many treasures. My Persian Sages are
wrapped in mats, but a couple of days of this weather and all
the Veronicas will be past hope. In an old book, The Farmer's
Calendar, the Balsam Poplar fence is strongly advised in damp,
loamy soil like mine. The method was to plant two rows of five-
foot saplings about four feet apart, each tree being set slanting
inward at an angle of forty-five degrees, so that each two trees
formed a V when looked at from the top of the row. When all
were set the tops were interlaced or plaited into a flat surface,
and the base of the trees set with sweetbriar slips, both poplar
shoots and sweet briar being clipped to shape as they grew. "This
fence" says the author, "if properly grown and clipped yearly shall
become so close so as not to suffer a fowl to creep through. It is
the most impenetrable as well as the most beautiful that can be
conceived." In situations too damp for beech fences I think this
might be worth a trial.[19]

The winter of 1936 gave way to the spring of 1937 and Lilias always delighted in
every aspect of new growth which started in the country much earlier and more
subtly than in urban areas:

With the uprush of the sap into the thickened branches the
enormous urge of life towards futurity is on us. Nature's ways
in spring are not all beauty and poetic rapture, she has far too
much creative force and drive, and the robustness of her methods
sometimes partakes of the bawdy. She seizes all living things,
fuses and conceives and creates, willingly if possible, if not with
violence, murder, rape, and destruction. But the spawn of these

[18]   LRH, Norfolk Life, 112.
[19]   Ibid, 125.

convulsions is always fecundity, life and yet more life, struggling
out and upward, into the warmth of the mounting sun.[20]

In May the cold weather returned; she and Ted Seago followed the Point-to-
Points at Flixton, a village two miles south west of Bungay in the Waveney valley.
point-to-points were races run by the local hunt or hunt club. Although Lilias,
like her father, abjured fox-hunting and dreaded the coming of the otter hunt to
the Bungay area, but she did not protest against hunting and evidently enjoyed
the country sports that were a by-product of it.

In between her detailed observations of nature, Lilias was also turning her
mind to dissect literature and fiction. She was impressed with Marguerite Steen's
Matador because a woman author had successfully presented a male point of
view.[21] She felt that Sheila Kaye-Smith had a similar gift. It was a talent that her
father remarked upon as unusual.[22] He never seems to have commented on the
male writer's ability, or otherwise, to enter the female mind. Having written
She perhaps he felt he had proved himself. One of Lilias' favourite writers was
Winifred Holtby, author of the best-selling and posthumously published *South
Riding*.[23] Holtby was a friend and contemporary of Vera Brittain and as a
journalist and columnist may have been something of a career-model for Lilias;
but Holtby had embraced socialism and pacifism which were never options for
Lilias, immersed as she was in the Haggard patriarchal world-view. Feminism was
another matter; Lilias was obviously interested in women's roles and women's
emancipation without ever espousing the cause. She read Margery Lawrence's *We
Write as Women*, a review of many women writers and their psychology, with great
interest but drew no particular conclusions for herself.[24] Although she wrote
and produced plays for the children of the family (Nada remembers Red Leg the
Pirate and Bluebeard) Lilias' attempts at fictional stories stayed in the bottom
of a drawer but there is no doubt she would have liked to move in that direction
if she could have developed her skills.[25] Meanwhile her interest in agriculture
and science prevailed. She noticed the precise location and condition of plants

20   Ibid, 145.
21   Marguerite Steen (1894–1975) was a dance teacher and prolific novelist, the
      lover of Sir William Nicholson the painter.
22   Sheila Kaye-Smith (1887–1956) a novelist and journalist much concerned with
      rural life and the changing role of women.
23   Winifred Holtby (1898–1935) journalist and author, served in the Women's
      Army Auxiliary Corps in France during WWI and afterwards met Vera Brittain
      while they were both studying at Oxford.
24   *Norfolk Notebook*, 169. Margery Lawrence (1889–1969) a writer of fantasy and
      detective fiction.
25   There are some plays and fictional material among her papers in the Cheyne
      Collection but no sign of a start of a novel although she mentions it in a letter
      to Margaret.

and wondered why they grew in one place and not another; and her knack with wild animals and birds extended to taming the tench in a lily pond — they ate from her hand.[26] She decided to grow hay in the front paddock where it had not been grown for twenty years. All advice was against her and all the hand tools needed had long since been dispersed. But her determination won out, and hay was indeed grown at Ditchingham again. There is an echo here of her father's success at growing a profitable crop of hay in Natal.

In between amusing descriptions of the trials of cider-making, she railed against the despoiling of the countryside by people without foresight or imagination. She defended the reputation of the lowly newt as a "merry little person" and said, "When you pick him up you hold part of the story of the creation in the hollow of your hand, for, like the wood-louse, he is an antique type."[27] As winter approached and the herring fleets made for home, Margaret was looking for a weekend cottage in the Cley area.

The country prepared for the coronation of George VI and Lilias celebrated the saving of the coastal area north of Stiffkey valley by the National Trust. She was aware that the author of *Tarka the Otter*, the famous Henry Williamson, had moved from Devon to Norfolk. Already an established writer and broadcaster, much influenced by Richard Jeffries,[28] Williamson was a close friend of Richard de la Mare, an editor at Faber. He had been de la Mare's best man at his marriage to Catherine Donaldson , a painter with connections to East Runton in Norfolk. Richard de la Mare's brother-in-law, Jack Donaldson,[29] was involved in supporting the left-wing Peckham Health Centre experiment which pioneered encouraging good health rather than just treating disease. To this end, from 1935, the Centre had its own organic farm. Richard de la Mare was inspired by this new thinking and commissioned a whole range of Faber books on the countryside and farming and was instrumental in promoting the organic movement.

Williamson arrived in May 1937 with his family (his wife Loetitia was known as "Gypsy") in a horse drawn caravan and a trailer pulled by a lorry to take possession of the derelict Old Hall Farm at Stiffkey. Williamson had no experience of farming; this, like Peckham, was an experiment. He was intent on reclaiming British agriculture as a symbol of national regeneration. It was part of his political agenda as a right-wing idealist.

According to biographer Daniel Farson, Williamson bought the property —

---

[26]   LRH, *Norfolk Life*, 187.
[27]   Ibid, 197.
[28]   Richard Jeffries, (1848–1887), a nature writer famous for *Bevis* (1882) and *The Story of my Heart* (1883).
[29]   Later Lord Donaldson of Kingsbridge and a Labour minister in the 1970s.

250 acres for £2,500 — because it included Old Hall Farm and six cottages.[30] It was the beginning of eight years of "unremitting slog" for his whole family. Williamson wrote about the work in a weekly column for the *Daily Express* and edited a full account in *The Story of a Norfolk Farm* published in 1941 by Faber. Williamson spotted Lilias' column in the *Eastern Daily Press* and was captivated by her knowledge and descriptions of the coastal area where he lived. He soon discovered her identity and made contact. It was to be a significant association for Lilias' career.

Preservationists were not the only cultural movement concerned with landscape and Englishness.[31] Organicist ideas that had been "galvanised by war and disappointed by peace" found expression in a variety of interest groups: Kinship in Husbandry founded by Gerard Wallop, Viscount Lymington[32] (from 1943, Earl of Portsmouth); The English Mistery [sic] a group with monarchist and rural allegiances from which a break-away group, The English Array, pursued a "back-to-the-land" agenda, again under the leadership of Viscount Lymington. Amongst the archaic chivalry and anti-modernism, there was also the developing science of ecology and a search for a new political order based on regions and a matching economic structure. Many followers on this path were convinced of the evils of usury that separated money from the soil and from labour — often a thinly veiled anti-Semitism. The naturalist John Hargreave broke with the Boy Scouts to found Kibbo Kift in 1920 which was especially interested in saving endangered animal and bird species. Five years later a splinter group called the Woodcraft Folk was formed. Hargreaves became persuaded of the benefits of Social Credit as an alternative monetary system and Kibbo Kift became the Green Shirt Movement for Social Credit.

These politicised organisations overlapped into rural polemics. At the end of the First World War Rider had been fired with anti-communist enthusiasm; he was briefly chairman of the short-lived Liberty League which quickly merged into the National Propaganda Movement.[33] The *Daily Herald* in March 1920 lampooned both Rider and Kipling:

> "Every Bolsh is blackguard,"
> Said Kipling to Haggard.
> "And given to tippling,"

---

[30] *Henry, An Appreciation of Henry Williamson* (London, Michael Joseph; 1982) ,105/6.
[31] D. Matless, *Landscape and Englishness*, 103.
[32] Although educated at Winchester and Balliol, he had been brought up on his parents' farm in Wyoming. Later he farmed in Hampshire.
[33] D.S. Higgins, *Rider Haggard The Great Storyteller* (London: Cassell, 1981), 236.

Said Haggard to Kipling.
"And a blooming outsider,"
Said Rudyard to Rider
"Their domain is a blood-yard"
Said Rider to Rudyard.

"That's just what I say,"
Said the author of *They*.
"I agree. I agree".
Said the author of *She*.

There was a wide range of right wing views amongst landowners and aristocrats. Lord Lothian, who owned a vast estate at Blickling north of Norwich, was a central figure in the Cliveden Set and a high-profile "appeaser".[34] The British Fascisti had been founded in 1923 by Mrs Rotha Linton-Orman, a member of the landed gentry, in order to campaign against communism. Julie V. Gottlieb in her *Feminine Fascism* noted that:

> Right-wing women emerged from their wartime experiences with
> a renewed sense of patriotic endeavour, and during the 1920s the
> BF was not alone among those organisations which gave vent to
> women's profound dread of communism. [35]

Dorothy, Viscountess Downe was a daughter of Sir William ffolkes of Hillington Hall near Lynn — the same ffolkes who had given at talk at St Felix School. She had married into the Dawnay family of Knapton Hall in Yorkshire but when she inherited Hillington she ran it herself without an agent. She was nominated as a prospective BF parliamentary candidate but never had the opportunity to stand in an election. In the mid-1930s she joined Mosley's British Union of Fascists and visited Germany. Social activities were frequent in the British Fascisti and Viscount and Viscountess Downe were two of the patrons of a "Mi Careme" ball at the Hotel Cecil in 1926. She was a great fund-raiser for and financial contributor to the BUF. She brought Oswald Mosley, the British fascist leader, to speak at a garden party at Hillington, and was intimate with his followers in the Mitford family. When war came Hillington Hall was searched by the police but Dorothy Dawnay was never interned, perhaps because she was so well-connected; she had been a lady-in-waiting to Queen Mary and a Deputy Lieutenant for the County of

---

[34]   Blickling became the first house to be owned by the National Trust. See James
       Lees-Milne's memoirs.
[35]   Julie V. Gottleib, *Feminine Fascism* (London and New York: I.B. Tauris; 2003),
       14.

Norfolk.[36] MI5 papers quoted on a BBC News website indicate that she actually wanted to be interned and become a martyr to the cause.[37] Although she was said to have "for some time almost entirely supported the National Fascists out of her own pocket" she was not involved in the organisational aspects of the movement. Files in the National Archives suggest that the government didn't want to arrest too many aristocrats since it would give Fascism a glamorous profile; but in this case they seemed to regard Dorothy Dawnay as rather stupid.[38] Dawnay, who saw herself not as a traitor but a great patriot, later withdrew her support — until after the war.

Most of the literary heavyweights of the 1930s were on the political left. Cecil Day Lewis (1904–1972), who is grouped with the "Oxford poets" which included W. H. Auden, was a passionate admirer of Thomas Hardy and wrote sensually of the English countryside. He was a member of the Communist Party during the 1930s and his poetry identifies nature and the land with the common people but also, as Janet Montefiore has pointed out, with a maternal fertility that will be "harmoniously subjected to masculine toil". His communist views didn't prevent implicit sexism in Day Lewis' imagery. He used "a sexist and imperialist trope that opposes a feminised or savage nature to European male knowledge and applied power".[39]

It was into this newly politicised awareness of English landscape and climate of cultural uncertainty that Lilias brought her affirmations of country life.

[36] Ibid, 296
[37] http://news.bbc.co.uk/go/pr/fr/-/1/hi/england/norfolk/4775682.stm – accessed 01/02/2010
[38] KV_2/2146 – releases of 2006
[39] Janet Montefiore, Men and Women Writers of the 1930s, (London and New York: Routledge, 1996), 111.

8

Natural Texts

During 1938 Lilias was working on a new book that was to be called *The Rabbit Skin Cap*. Once again it was written in a voice not her own with Lilias acting as mediator and midwife. She had persuaded George Baldry to record memories of his boyhood in Bungay and Ditchingham.

His father had been one of seven renowned, and sometimes infamous, shoemakers or "snobs" and he himself had learned carpentry and building. Baldry lived up the river from the Bath House in what had been the Old Mill from where he let out boats. The cottage had belonged to his parents and he often worked on the Haggard estate helping with building projects and supplying seasoned materials; he was a regular character in Lilias' weekly diaries.

Lilias used the format she had developed for *I Walked by Night*: the life story interleaved with an eclectic mix of country lore and verse and once again she asked Edward Seago to create the

The Mill House stood on the banks of the River Waveney.

Seago's illustration of the Old Mill, from The Rabbit Skin Cap.

illustrations. The original manuscript of Baldry's life story is in Bungay Museum.

The public appetite for country or rural books was gaining ground. The young writer Julian Tennyson was collecting material for a book on Suffolk and came to visit Lilias in the summer of 1938. She took him to see Burgh Castle where they tried to imagine what Roman life in the area would have been like forty-six years before the birth of Christ. Tennyson's book *Suffolk Scene* was published by Faber the following year. In other parts of the country too, the trend was taking hold. G. Henry Warren, a journalist and author inspired by Richard Jefferies, was a prolific recorder of country life in the north of England. It was he who came up with the phrase *"The Good Life"* for the title of a book in 1946 – a title which bequeathed the whole concept of "back-to-the-land" to the post-war period and eventually to television. Doreen Wallace, of tithe war fame, was herself a novelist of the countryside. H.W. Freeman's novels set in Suffolk included *Down in the Valley*, which offered country life as an antidote to psychological and physical malaise.

War with Germany now seemed inevitable; Lilias described the threat as specifically from the personality of Hitler. She quoted the eminent medical man, Lord Horder who had said, "What matter the colour of men's shirts if they are so soon to be their shrouds?"[1]

In early September Lilias took the twelve-year-old Nada up to the coast for a holiday before school started. Once again she noted the sadness of the Michaelmas farm sales but again without making any political inference.[2] Travelling through Norwich Lilias saw that Chapelfield Gardens had been "scored across with trenches and piled with earth, wood, and corrugated iron" in preparation for invasion.[3] Dolly's son, Archie Cheyne, married Marie-Louise Brett but with all the preparations for war affecting the armed services only one member of the family was able to attend the ceremony and wish him luck.

The horrors of the First World War came flooding back to Lilias – "things most of us have spent twenty years trying to forget". She remembered "the dear companions with whom one picnicked and danced and laughed …and who lie in those flower-bright gardens in France and Belgium." She asked on their behalf: is it for this – another war – that they had "suffered unimagined miseries, and caused those who loved [them] to suffer them also?"[4]

Then on September 30th 1938 news of the reprieve came – the Munich Pact brought "the feeling of vast relief" and release from the nightmare. Lilias moved into the Bath House for the autumn but by Armistice Day she was remembering again the horrors of the past and of her visit to the battlefields in 1925 – the Menin Road, Passchendaele and the "shell-torn salient."[5]

Nada was attending St Felix School as a boarder and Lilias visited the establishment for the first time since she had left. She recalled how difficult she had found the experience of attending school since "at nearly sixteen it was far too late to catch up with the work or be really broken to the routine which was

1 LRH, *Norfolk Notebook,* 28.
2 Ibid, 45.
3 Ibid, 33.
4 Ibid, 32.
5 Ibid, 49.

entirely strange to me." At Nada's confirmation service the Bishop preached on the difficulties lying ahead for the young people but Lilias thought that for some children schooldays were the hardest days of their lives. She recalled the vast gap that used to exist between young people and their parents because of the upper class habit of keeping young people in the school room, sometimes still eating dinner there into their early twenties. She herself looked back and thought she had lived in a different world to the adults.[6] Perhaps she was also describing a feeling of disconnection.

In January of 1939 gales, snow and rain battered East Anglia for twenty-four hours resulting in heavy flooding. The bridge into Bungay was swept away. George Baldry recalled, philosophically, that the floods of 1877 had been worse. The clearing up process was arduous both domestically and for the church and parish councils.

In March the Council for the Preservation of Rural England arranged an exhibition at Norwich Castle. As an active member Lilias went to the opening and took the opportunity to write about the disfiguring of beauty spots by advertising hoardings and the lack of awareness of wherein the beauty of landscape lies. She also aired the anxieties of how high streets were being ruined by the insertion of shop windows in ancient houses and by speculative building.

The production of *The Rabbit Skin Cap* was now well under way and Lilias visited the village school to find a boy to model for Seago's pictures of the young Baldry for the coloured jacket and frontispiece. The book's editor together with Ted Seago and the publisher, Collins, came to visit her in the Bath House in the spring of 1939 to hammer out details.

About this time Geoffrey Christian, Lady Haggard's godson, made his way to the centre of Lilias' life. Geoffrey and his brother Jack were adventurous spirits, gentlemen of fortune. Lately Geoffrey had been in Argentina where Dan Haggard (son of Alfred and an engineer) had given him a job managing all the cattle for his firm. Now, recently divorced and having lost a lung to tuberculosis, Geoffrey was in need of a place to convalesce; Lilias took him in. He was a romantic, swashbuckling figure and Lilias seems to have been much taken with him although Dan, in a later letter,[7] said, somewhat enigmatically, that Geoffrey was his own worst enemy. From a series of photographs of the period he seems to have enjoyed at least a long summer in Norfolk.

Lilias' thoughts turned often to the possibilities ahead. For what, she asked in her column, do men fight — other than conviction or duty? Her answer was that they fought for the ideal of the land that was home. "For the memory of arable

6   Ibid, 52 and 53.
7   Letter to Margaret Spurrell. Cheyne Collection.

Top left: *Geoffrey Christian outside Margaret's caravan.* Top right: *Lilias, Geoffrey, Margaret and an unknown man picnicing outside Margaret's caravan.* Bottom left: *Lilias perched on Geoffrey's knees.* Bottom right: *Lilias with Geoffrey.* All Cheyne Collection.

fields under a windswept sky; the fall of a valley to the river; the green stretch of pastures where they sweep up to meet the woods or the bare-blue-misted hills. The place where they have been born or have been happy, or own some acres of earth. That is where our roots really lie, in our own place."[8] She began making preparations by digging up land to grow more potatoes. Kitty Athill "came down to discuss the registration of the car for national service, and the suggestion I should do "accounts" in connection with the child-evacuation scheme, which moved me to unseemly mirth, my abilities regarding anything mathematical being about on a par with the average child of six."[9] She described the day to day tension and then resorted to quoting from *The Religion of Taoism* about the wisdom of not waging war.

[8]   LRH, *Norfolk Notebook*, 104.
[9]   Ibid, 110.

The summer of 1939 was hot and lovely. Lilias visited Blythburgh and Walberswick then down to Sussex to stay with a friend who farmed there. On her return Abbot and Kathleen, the graduates of the Rhodesian Fairbridge farm who been in living in America for seven years, came to stay and they tried to persuade Lilias to take a trip to "this great America which is so nearly allied to us". Abbot was teaching history at an American college; Lilias and Margaret took their visitors to see Binham Priory and the vast Tudor East Barsham Manor that had once belonged to the Paston family.

As summer waned the galley proofs of *The Rabbit Skin Cap* arrived; they were a month late but Lilias was greatly relieved to actually see her work in print. Having prepared the Bath House for a new tenant, she settled down to make corrections. "A thunderstorm had cleared the air, a relief from the endless hot and blustering gale which has worried us for weeks."[10] One afternoon sitting on the hill-side at Ditchingham collecting wild thyme for a friend's pot-pourri Lilias watched her cousin Dick, who lived in the Lodge, walking slowly up the hill: "with long spud stick and the familiar hunch of the shoulders, time seemed to leap backwards a generation, and I saw myself in faded blue overall and short legs, toiling behind. So heart-twisting is that family resemblance to my father, so alike and yet so different. Half a generation has gone since the master of this land walked up the slope of the hill on a summer evening."[11] This was how she still saw her father — "the master of this land".

A few days later Lilias went up to London where the roads were "crowded with Army lorries, guns, and troops . . . while overhead squadron upon squadron of aeroplanes roared and dipped and banked and sped away into the distance."[12] She was called rapidly home by a telegram to say that Dick Haggard had died. Nada and Joy Turner had been with him when he had a fit and fell into the Waveney and although they had gone for help they had been unable to save him from drowning. He was, in effect, a late casualty of the 1914–18 war. The funeral made Lilias look back and wonder at the passing of the landed gentry as a class. "it is a new and, we are told, an infinitely better world, and so in the arrogance of one's young days, scorning all things Victorian, I was inclined to believe. Now, turning over old letters and diaries, hearing old tales of our grandfathers from those who, from their station in life, bore the brunt of its hardships — I sometimes wonder if it is."[13]

On September 1st 1939 the Nazis marched into Poland and two days later Neville Chamberlain declared war. Lilias called it:

10   Ibid, 134.
11   Ibid, 137.
12   Ibid, 138.
13   Ibid, 140.

A Sunday few of us will ever forget, the end of long hopes, anxieties, and fears . . . What many of us have faced once in our youth, we must now face for a second time in middle life, but with this difference. This time we know to the full what war — with all its profound miseries and suffering — means, and are without the unquestioning faith and enthusiasm which believed so implicitly that no sacrifice was too great, because once victory was achieved we should build a brave new world where peace was the only password. . . . We can only, in the words of the bible, gird up our loins, and thankful if we are still sound in wind and limb, do what first comes to hand, remembering always that immortal question: "Who dies if England lives?"[14]

There was an immediate influx of evacuated children and mothers with young babies from London to the countryside and Ditchingham was no exception. Lilias wrote,

I was slightly appalled at the obvious inability of most London women to adapt themselves to the country. The fact they have to walk, that gas does not come out of a pipe, or water out of a tap, that they may occasionally be left alone with their children, that the shops are a mile or more away, that they see the fields ahead instead of streets, and above all the silence, "as if one were sleeping with the dead", as a depressed female remarked, one and all strike dismay to their hearts. If they can stand it — and I doubt very much if the majority can — it will be one of the wonders which national unity and endeavour, coupled with personal sacrifice, can work in times of stress in this astonishing nation of ours.[15]

Lilias was not alone in her shock at the attitude of the evacuees. David Matless in *Landscape and Englishness* assessed the reaction to the upheaval:

Whatever its social variety, public debate addressed evacuation as a working-class movement into the country. Citizen and anti-citizen walked abroad once more.[16]

The "anti-citizen" was the person who could not see the "real" rural England. Evacuation produced class confrontation on the Home Front. Assessing the options, people with large country houses were often quick to offer them to private schools. The pupils of St Felix School were evacuated to Cornwall.

14   Ibid, 141.
15   Ibid, 142.
16   D. Matless, *Landscape and Englishness*, 180.

Matless quotes the Women's Institute booklet on *Town Children through Country Eyes* : "many of the guests arrived in a condition and with modes of life or habits which were startlingly less civilized than those they [the country people] had accepted for a life-time."[17] This refers to an estimated ten per cent of the children who were verminous, unclean, rude and apparently unhouse-trained with regard to the use of lavatories.

Most of them quickly returned back to London within months.[18] A report in the January 26th 1940 edition of the *Eastern Daily Press* said that 315,192 of the 734,883 unaccompanied children had returned home. Of the 260,276 accompanied children, 223,381 had returned home; and of the 166,206 mothers, 145,681 had returned. The experiment was evidently far from being a success, particularly with the adult women — although the keeping of data seems to have been exemplary.

In one swift national exercise the convictions of all those country writers who had been advocating the spiritual and physical benefits of living close to the land were brought into a different focus. It might (and did) do well for some, but for slum children and the city-born mother of small children the isolation and hardships of the country had little to offer; was this proof of national urban malaise or prejudicial idealism on the part of rural writers? For some, such as a Polish woman who had escaped from Germany barely a week before with three little children, with no language and no kosher food, the experience of rural Norfolk was one of deep distress.

Out of this, as Matless points out, via a variety of social surveys including that by the Women's Institute, the rural mothers suddenly (and somewhat irrationally) attained moral elevation. They could sew, knit, cook and turn their hand to a multiplicity of tasks while their urban equivalents were labelled indolent and unskilled, or working mothers with little interest in domesticity and bored by country life. It seems now that little thought was given to a transition period of acclimatising; people seem to have been expected to change their ways instantly. Over the years since the war, stories have emerged from adults who recall this first childhood taste of country life as a positive and beneficial experience that lasted, although for all of them there was the trauma of separation from their families. There have also been stories of loneliness, anxiety, misery and abuse including sexual abuse.

Looking ahead to petrol rationing Lilias quickly acquired a pony and cart. The problems of refugees, air raid shelters, black-out blinds, fuel and transport now became the topics of family discussion. Angie and Brownie (Miss Brown,

17   Ibid, 181.
18   Ibid, 143.

Nada's governess, still living with them) learned how to ride bicycles while Lilias assessed the production of fruit and vegetables and the replacement of her fuel-hungry hob in the Bath House. "Everyone cheerfully preparing to live an infinitely simpler and more restricted life, in which the willing co-operation of those who supply our daily needs is no small help."[19]

Lilias, as she surveyed the landscape continued to marvel at the generosity and splendour of the natural world. Faced with the likelihood of a winter "rationed, blacked out, and transportless" she looked on the bright side and considered she might spend the extra time resuscitating old writing projects — a pantomime, an historical novel begun in her youth and plans for a history of the big houses and families in the district. In the latter case she had a collaborator who would provide the gossipy secrets — was that Margaret? Any research notes or manuscript have disappeared.

In her weekly column Lilias continued to chronicle the cycle of the year:

> We started to pick the Blenheim Oranges. A fair crop of this wonderful old apple, which is a hundred years the senior of its only rival, Cox's Orange. Somehow new trees do not bear apples the same flavour as the old ones, and many people have assured me there is a modern variety which is not so good. … Apples like flowers and trees have their fashion. Where are the Juneatings, Soon-Ripe-Sweetings, the Ladies' Longing, the Honeymeal or the less delicately named Great Belly and Sweet Snout, Cat's Head or Go-No-Further; well known when Blenheim was born. In deep old gardens or deserted farm orchards some hoary trees may perhaps bear fruit, still sweet as their long-forgotten names.[20]

The bureaucracy of war began to permeate village life. The Ditchingham Parish Church council was called to the "Mission Room" quickly converted to a First-Aid Post, to receive instructions. Lilias was apoplectic about the arrangements that required her, in the event of an air raid, to report with her car to convey the injured "to some distant place not yet revealed". However, although the Red Cross requested that the Fuel Officer supply her with fuel for this purpose he adamantly refused saying that she must collect it from a depot nine miles away. But her ration of eight gallons was only enough for her immediate household needs and nothing was allowed for her to go any further. She therefore concluded, somewhat contrarily, that when the sirens sounded she could peacefully stay in bed.[21]

It was into these unpromising times that *The Rabbit Skin Cap* was published

[19]   LRH, *Norfolk Notebook,* 145.
[20]   Ibid, 153.
[21]   Ibid, 161.

in late October 1939 as a "Tale of a Norfolk countryman's youth written in his old age by George Baldry, edited by Lilias Rider Haggard, illustrated by Edward Seago". Lilias introduced the work as something which falls outside of most readers' experience:

> What is written here has nothing to do with cities or those who live in them. Nothing to do with books or the written word, for

Edward Seago's frontispiece for The Rabbit Skin Cap

most of the men and women who people its pages could neither read nor write, and these things touched their lives but lightly.[22]

The subject of the book is a man who differed from his contemporaries because, as Lilias puts it :

> …he was born with a mechanical brain. Denied its proper outlet one sees, again and again, how it strove for expression. His endless curiosity as to how things were made. His unchildlike patience in conquering the problems of braiding and netting and eel-trap making, his passion for tools and woodwork, his absorption in methods, his desire to always try something new.[23]

The essence of it was that George Baldry was a clever, talented boy born into an impoverished and largely ignorant, but spirited, country family with little or no access to practical training or education. He was left-handed at a time when teachers forced their pupils to use the right hand for writing [all quotes are in the vernacular text] :

> It was easy there [for the teacher] to see if I used my left hand, but one day when I thought she weren't looking I changed the pencil over and soon had my copy done. Teacher sees and calls out:
> "Put that pencil in your right hand, young Baldry, if I catch you using your left again I'll give you the cane." And I says:
> "My mother uses her left hand, why shan't I?"
> I didn't make much progress using my right hand my copy was allus being crossed off, so whenever I see a chance I'd slip the pencil into my left hand, keeping one eye on the teacher, and soon she twigged me. She called out for me to come down from the gallery as she had something to show me, so of course I was down in a crack, and only when she pulled out the cane I see what it was I was to see. Twisting up her lip she told me to hold out my hand and down it came but I was quicker and the cane came down on her knee. Then she got the wind up – called one of the assistants to hold me – and she caught my wrist and let me have it – one – two – three – four, and some extra to make up for the one she missed. Then there was a storm of tears and blubbering – the rest of the Class sat as quiet as mice – and the teacher took no more notice, feeling sure I wouldn't use my left again. Nor did I, for it was so sore and tingling for days after it

22   *The Rabbit Skin Cap,* 7.
23   *The Rabbit Skin Cap,* 7/8.

cured me for life of writing with it, though there's many a job to
this day I'd sooner use my left hand for.[24]

Baldry's father, Happy Jack, was a "character" in the Bungay area — one of
seven shoemakers who supplemented their meagre income by poaching and
were known for their brawling and drinking. Baldry is unapologetic for their
misdemeanours:

> If their ways were looked at in the right light they were made
> what they had become, getting only a bread and cheese living —
> the cheese hard to see sometimes — and also there is a saying,
> "Get old — get artful".[25]

There was never enough money to feed and clothe the family — although his
father seems to have had enough money for the pub.

> Salt sop was a few pieces of bread crumbled into a basin with
> small pieces of butter, lard, or dripping with hot water poured
> over, the water dipped up out of the river, making sop like good
> broth with bubbles of fat floating on top. We didn't know good
> from bad and the latter being mostly our share we were happy
> and contented. My brother got fat on it but I was that poor and
> skinny I was nick-named "Bones." If my parents could have fed us
> better they would have done, but we had to live on what ever we
> could get.[26]

Casual cruelty was commonplace and the descriptions of his father taking a
belt to George and his brother after they had picked a neighbour's flowers are
likely to stay imprinted on the reader's mind as acutely as the actual beating did
on George's:

> Being eighteen months older than my brother I was considered
> the worst of the two, but I coiled as close as I could against the
> wall, my brother in front, so he got most of it across his sit-me-
> down-on. Father couldn't get me according to his liking, so he
> reached forrard, caught me by the back of the neck and swung
> me into the middle of the planshard [boarded floor], as though I
> were a spinning top, and give me a troshing so I remember every
> detail of that evening to this day. Mother tried her best to save us,
> but to stop him in one of those rages would be like trying to stop
> the wind. He'd started and meant to finish. We kicked up such

[24]   Ibid, 59/60.
[25]   Ibid, 131.
[26]   Ibid, 34.

a row Mrs Easthaugh hear and come a-running begging him to stop, crying she wish she'd never said a word about the flowers, and Father turned on her with:

"Du you think I am goin' to have them up to tricks like that, they'll git me inter a proper muddle if I don't look to it. I'm going to be Master and have my lads do what I want, not what they like. I'll make 'em mind now they're young. An old Man used to be telling me bend the twig while green, Jack, and I find what he says is right. If they do as they choose now — dang me — they'll be kicking my legs later and I'll square 'em up now I've got the chance, and if you wimmen hinders me, I'll serve yer all alike."

So there was one lesson learned, and we did not forget that dose of strap oil nor what it would given for, and maybe 'twas the better for us as the lesson was sharp.[27]

In the small community of Bungay and its satellite villages the Baldrys gave as good as they got and George's mother was ready to defend her boys with her tongue as when a farmer tried to do them out of payment in kind:

I'll pull yer limb from limb you long lanky lout you, if you don't leave my boys alone. Git off my medder — they ain't yer swedes — you sold 'em and you begruges the poor boys a swede when they have they been working like blacks [sic] this two days to help Shepherd. You don't care if the pot boil fat or lean, wait till my husband gits at yer, he'll make you wish you'd niver been born, you old hike.[28]

As with *I Walked by Night*, Lilias vouched for the "truth of the story" in that all the locations remain unchanged and the author himself was still at work and

…his workshops filled with the unimaginable collection of wood and iron work which has given him his nickname of "Old Iron". The place where three generations of children from my family have gone with the familiar plea, "Please, George, could you mend this for me?"[29]

As for her aim, she turns again to the preservation of something that is vanishing, so that a piece of English countryside history shall not be lost for ever, nor the memory of the Seven Famous Snobs who in their youth ran, and poached, and worked, and fought, in this corner of a simpler and a younger England.[30]

"Simpler and younger" —   this hankering after something "lost" was

27 *The Rabbit Skin Cap*, 53/54.
28 Ibid, 36.
29 Ibid, 8.
30 Ibid, 9.

symptomatic of much writing of the post-WWI period.[31] Nostalgia is also common to women who are psychologically caught in the spell of their father's gaze.[32]

By trial and error and taking any opportunity that came along, young Baldry learned a wide variety of country skills - how to make eel traps, how to look after livestock, how to make bricks, how to lure pheasants and hide from the law, how to cut hay, how to thatch and eventually

George Baldry in older age. Cheyne Collection.

carpentry which became his trade. All these learning processes he recounted anecdotally in dialect including the characters and incidents that surrounded them.

In amongst the hard work, illness, bad weather and poverty there were fairs on the common, horse races, high jinks and for the men the numerous attractions of the pubs. It is a seductive experience for the reader — being given access to a lost world.

At the age of eleven, sitting quietly in the corner of the Golden Cross public house at Mendham, listening to his elders, young George heard something that gave him a guiding star in his life. They were talking about a chap who had tried to discover the secret of perpetual motion and build a machine to demonstrate it.[33] This idea stayed with George all his life and gave him a mental objective as well as a hobby for his spare time.

Baldry fell in love when he was still a boy and eventually married that very same sweetheart, but not until late in his and her life which gives poignancy to his memoir — rather in reverse to the experience of Rolfe:

> She did not want asking twice, and the difficulties that had all along been in the way were gone, so we agreed to start off in double harness, and got married on 1 October 1922.
>
> If I had my time over again I would do that same thing the early side of twenty. As it was if I had waited any longer I should've missed what she had to give me — the sunshine and comfort of

[31]   Essay by Claire Buck "This Other Eden" in *Women's Experience of Modernity 1875–1945*, edited by Ann Ardis and Leslie W. Lewis (Baltimore: Johns Hopkins University Press, 2003), 70.

[32]   See *Father's Daughters*, especially pages 12/13.

[33]   *The Rabbit Skin Cap*, 101.

my life. I have found again and again it is a true saying — that
delays are dangerous.[34]

One of the saddest aspects of Baldry's memories is the scarcity of social
support or loyalty amongst the country poor. He describes being cheated and
maltreated by farmers when he was a boy.[35] So often it was every man — or every
boy — for himself and misfortune was often the object of ridicule. Everyone knew
what fate ultimately had in store:

> At that time there was no old age pension and old folk had
> to work as long as they could crawl, or else go to the Spike or
> workhouse, and kept their house together till the last.[36]

People would live in any kind of abject misery to avoid it and hope to die first.
George Baldry was lucky enough to find a trade he loved and enjoyed his deep
knowledge of woodwork. He finished the book with a few lines that, given his
hardships, are haunting in their humility:

> I write these last words of the story of my boyhood as I wrote the
> first, to the sound of Bungay bells chiming over the common.
> Through childhood, youth, and manhood, and all the troublous
> ways of a man's life the Lord has kept me, and in his peace, mercy
> and kindness I abide in my old age.[37]

The book was modestly noted by the *Eastern Daily Press* on Monday 6th
November 1939 with a short article on page three describing the contents and
implying that "only those who love Norfolk and know its country folk will"
appreciate it.

It was a very cold winter and Lilias, even at this stage, was, unlike her colleagues
on the Refugee Committee, pessimistic about both the duration and the severity
of the war. She thought herself realistic. She had listened to Mr Churchill and
taken note of his tone:

> One may in the past have mistrusted that brilliant versatile brain,
> that swift wit, that immense and all-embracing vision which saw
> obstacles only as leaves to be swept away before the whirlwind of
> national enterprise. But what a relief in this war, which has given us
> so many polite phrases, so much involved diplomacy, such a mass of
> official tact, to hear a little plain speaking. To have our skeleton in the
> cupboard — another world war — danced before us stripped of the
> petticoats with which we have striven so long to clothe it. It is not a

34   Ibid, 256.
35   Ibid, 209.
36   Ibid, 226.
37   Ibid, 257.

pleasant sight. It grins and jibbers and its bones rattle, but it is none
the less a salubrious and heartening thing to look it in the face, to call
our enemy openly by names Mr Churchill did not hesitate to use —
hate, murder, treachery, oppression , and cruelty, for those are the
things we are fighting against.[38]

Early in the New Year Lilias went up to London to record an interview at
the BBC — so it seems that her new book had found a keen audience outside of
Norfolk after all. Perhaps it was a case of the prophet in her own country.[39]

The Spurrell family estate at St Faith's had been requisitioned in 1939 for an
RAF airbase (later becoming Norwich airport) leaving Margaret homeless —
although not without means. She began looking for a new home along the north
Norfolk coast but the area was now "a district given over to the construction of
aerodromes, camps, gun emplacements and vast schemes of coastal defence".[40]
Eventually in January 1940 she and Lilias spotted a derelict cottage with a mature
orchard at Wiveton and Lilias persuaded a reluctant Margaret of its potential.
They spent many weekends working on the orchard and garden and supervising
the restoration and additions. Lilias also converted the cow shed built by Baldry
beside the Bath House into a cottage for Margaret's use.

The winter of 1940 was so cold that the swans and robins were dying of
starvation which was deeply distressing to Lilias. The shortage of wild food meant
that pigeons and pheasants stripped the vegetable gardens at Ditchingham of
winter greens. Then in February Lilias fell foul of the censors. Her February 12th
column implied that she has been told off for talking about the weather. It was
information that might, apparently, be useful to the enemy. Her "Countrywoman's
Diary" ended abruptly. Lilias and Margaret decided to take a holiday and headed
up to a favourite haunt, the Kirkcudbright area of Scotland, for bird-watching
and fly fishing. They left Norfolk swathed in furs and sheepskins and in Scotland
found temperatures in the 70s Fahrenheit; they spent their time roaming the hills
and absorbing the scenery and wildlife. On the way back they diverted to Haworth
in Yorkshire which Lilias, a great admirer of the Brontes, had longed to see for
many years even though Margaret called them "these tuberculous neurotics you
are so fond of".[41] However, the vicarage was difficult to find and the visit was not
altogether a success:

At last, as afternoon waned, up an incredibly steep street we

[38]   LRH,, *Norfolk Notebook*, 168.
[39]   She may have made a number of broadcasts including a talk for the *"This
England"* series for which there is a surviving manuscript in the Cheyne
Collection.
[40]   LRH, *A Country Scrapbook*, 23.
[41]   Ibid, 15.

found it. A notice directed us over a stile and across some fields, so hot, dirty and tea-less, but, still determined, we breasted the slope. The first field contained an emaciated horse and some ragged hens, existing apparently upon nothing; the second, three goats complaining to heaven having wound themselves to a standstill round their pegs, and a highly artistic fence composed of bedsteads. There was not a moor in sight, only apparently a slag heap bounded by the railway. The house! Could our eyes deceive us? It was like the worst type of Victorian villa.[1]

Coming back into Norfolk in May they found the tulips were out and the spring far advanced. When Lilias resumed her column in June it was no longer a diary but a "Country Notebook" often an essay on one subject, or less particular notes about her daily life. As a result the pieces are fuller and more discursive. The first ones were about her trip to Scotland and the visit to Haworth. Then they range widely in topic from "Around the House and Garden" to "Memoirs of Old London", "An XVIII Century Budget", "Bats in the Belfry" and making "A Reed Fence" and "Birdsongs".

Lilias was becoming an essayist.

[1]   Ibid, 15.

9

The Domain and the Boundaries

The war hit rural areas hard. While Lilias' articles allude to the shortages, the increasing officialdom and the bleakness of wartime Norfolk, they also paint deeply-felt and tightly-drawn pictures of the landscape that brought her a loyal following and crystallized her reputation. Her columns describing country life for the *Eastern Daily Press* were clipped out and sent by Norfolk families to servicemen all over the world as a reminder of everything for which they were fighting: "It is English Life — she is not writing for herself but for all of us."[1]

The landscape may have been real enough but "English Life" was becoming something of a myth, although a powerful one; the "life" the soldiers, sailors and airmen had left behind was rapidly changing under the stringency and demands of war. County War Agricultural Executive Committees were set up with lines of command from Whitehall through to Parish Councils. As Rider had predicted so many years before, the country's excessive dependence on imports for food would be a disaster in war time.[2] While the major cities suffered the mortalities and devastation of bombing, especially during the Blitz from early September 1940 to May 1941, the country endured a relentless, heavy battle: what was later called the "Land at War". Suddenly it became imperative to increase production, plough up every available acre and most importantly to mechanise farming. The war did what no amount of proselytising had achieved: the government at last took the land seriously. But it also took agriculture in the opposite direction to the organicists; far from developing natural methods and community farms the land was to become a factory for food production under the control and supervision of the government.

Italian prisoners of war from the Seething Prisoner of War camp worked in gangs down at the Bath House cutting down trees for pit props and at the Carr

---

[1]   Review from *The Sunday Times* quoted on the dust jacket of *A Norfolk Notebook,* (London: Faber & Faber, 1946).
[2]   LRH, *A Country Scrapbook* , 90–1, and HRH's *1914–25 Diaries.*

estate, Ditchingham Hall, they dug and cleared ditches. Lilias immersed herself in intensive market gardening, selling the extra produce on a weekly market stall in Bungay; the takings went towards financing a fishing trawler.

Lilias wrote about the various incidents and challenges they experienced. Refugees as well as evacuees stayed for short periods of time. Lilias and Kitty Carr had two cows between them which they kept for milk. A Hurricane aeroplane came down on the drive of Ditchingham House one night destroying the chicken run at the Gate House and killing the pilot, a boy from Nottingham. Reggie Cheyne contacted his family. Jam-making, with takings from the sales going to government funds, changed from being part of the seasonal household provision to becoming a patriotic imperative, thus acquiring a moral stature. All the Ditchingham House staff were eventually required for war work leaving the family to cope on their own with the huge house and its three hopelessly antiquated boilers and the estate. Lady Haggard and Miss Brown (Nada's former governess) escaped the threat of bombing and invasion by going to Cornwall for two years but came back in 1942 by which time Lady Haggard was increasingly frail. Nada had been evacuated to first Cornwall and then Somerset with the other pupils of St Felix School. On the plus side Lilias gained land girls to help her out.

The Women's Land Army had been set up at the outset of war with Lady Denman, the chair of the Women's Institute, at its head.[3] That alone signalled a no-nonsense approach but David Matless's research highlights the contemporary controversies of "naturalness and social acceptability"[4]. Mechanisation enabled the "feminization" of land work and according to Vita Sackville-West (the author of the history of *The Women's Land Army*) some women found their vocation through the work. Interestingly too, there were discussions of the genetic value of bringing new blood into isolated rural communities such as the Forest of Arden — and no doubt the remoter parts of Norfolk — where there had been intermarriage of just a few families for generations. The Nazis were not alone in their preoccupation with eugenics.

One of the land girls who came to work for Lilias was a young local woman, a Joan Tusting from Oulton Broad. Her family were builders' supply merchants and she had been attending Lowestoft Art School. She worked as a land girl for three years. She had been doing garden training in Bungay where Lilias spotted her pruning raspberries. She boarded in a cottage with a relative who had a daughter the same age and then went home at weekends. Lilias used to take her up to Wiveton to help pick fruit at Margaret's cottage.

Joan Tusting found Lilias very easy to get on with and helped her with more

3   Gertrude Denman, 1884–1954, a Liberal, a supporter of women's rights and
        wife of the fifth Governor-General of Australia.
4   D. Matless, 176.

than the gardening. Lilias would call her into her study and hand over her weekly copy for the *Eastern Daily Press* and ask Joan to take it on the Norwich bus. It was often at the last minute and Joan would have to run up the road after the bus. What arrangement was in place at the other end when the bus arrived is not recorded.

Joan kept her own boat at George Baldry's moorings and would walk across the marshes to take it out. Once she forgot the time and was late getting to the Bath House. Lilias became worried that she might have capsized — a moment of anxiety that she wrote about in her column. Joan was afraid her mother would read the piece and find out that she had been late for work. All the daily events went into Lilias' column. Joan, not knowing Ted Seago's sexual preferences, thought of him as Lilias' "fancy man" since he was part of the coterie with whom she went about.[5]

Margaret continued to renovate her cottage at Wiveton. This area of north Norfolk was now closed to tourists and casual visitors so that the tiny streets of Blakeney and the wide open marshes were deserted. Lilias and Margaret went up to pick apples from Margaret's orchard and inspect the progress on the house:

> The roof is on the two new rooms which were once shed and
> loft. No mean achievement, as, owing to timber restrictions,
> practically no new wood could be used. With the help of old
> timber and driftwood from the beach, they stand completed
> in the original flint cobble, almost a lost art except in parts of
> East Anglia. For new surrounds to doors and some other jobs
> I offered to find up a few short lengths of oak I had, originally
> some of thousands bought by my father for laying parquet
> floors.[6]

There were government regulations about almost everything; one of them was to clear inflammable materials from top floors of houses. Lilias began sorting out the attics at Ditchingham House and turned her mind to her ancestors and the excitable and imaginative temperament that had entered into the family via a Russian great grandmother and intermarriage with a Huguenot family in the eighteenth century.[7]

In the autumn, as she tackled the tasks of clearing the garden of old plants and debris, she ruminated on the importance of jettisoning old ideas in order to keep a healthy outlook. She quoted Winifred Holtby's "This alone is to be feared

5   Interview by the author with Miss Joan Tusting October 20th 2008 by
    telephone.
6   LRH, *A County Scrapbook*, 33.
7   Ibid, 31. The wealthy Meybohms, merchants of St Petersburg, were German
    Jews.

— the closed mind, the sleeping imagination, the death of the spirit. The death of the body is to that, I think, a little thing."[8] A year into the war she was finding the repetitive writing of condolence letters both heartrending and impossibly inadequate. She gave a talk to a coastal branch of the Women's Institute and on the homeward journey she and Margaret stopped to look over the marshes: a timeless, silent moment as they gazed at the "shadowy forms of the horses" moving softly along the dykes which was then broken by the "double-note hum" as an enemy bomber flew in across the coast.

Lilias with her nephew Mark Cheyne and Miss Brown, at the Bath House. Cheyne Collection.

Trapping moles and shooting rabbits in order to preserve the garden were perennial occupations. Shortages of butter and cheese led her to consider keeping a goat, although it was clear that no one else in the family would share the tasks of milking and caring for the animal. In one of her essays on "Children, Past and Present" she used the focus of old samplers of sewing stitches to look back at the children of yesteryear in her mother's family. Then, as she packed up the cottage in Blakeney which she had rented for five years, she thought of the many young relatives and friends who had been able to enjoy it as a base to sail, swim and bird-watch over the summers.

She and Margaret moved some of the contents to Margaret's house at Wiveton. Lilias described her attempt to give Margaret a dresser with a drawer full of bric-a-brac and Margaret's response which was to turn the drawer upside down on the floor saying, "all these things are perfectly useless…it's just hoarding…" forcing Lilias to meekly throw them all away. It is hard to imagine that Lilias was often this compliant.

Increasing restrictions on imports forced more and more self-sufficiency in rural areas. During the rains of a "long and bitter spring" in 1941 Lilias described the hand-sowing of oats and peas and the harrowing of the fields by horses; it was job that had been done by oxen in the past. Tractors had been used to bring marginal land into production and she observed that "the thoughtless neglect of twenty years must be caught up in two" by "overdosing the land with artificals"

8   Ibid, 40.

[fertilizers] — a policy that did not bode well for the future.[9]

At Easter of 1941 Lilias moved down to the Bath House in her seasonal progress. (It is often difficult to pinpoint which house she was living in at any given time. Her sisters also moved around.) She had lost two dogs since the previous spring and still missed them. Because of the need for economy this was the last period she spent at the Bath House until the end of the war.

After the harsh spring there was a sudden warm summer and the crops ripened quickly in the heat — hay, grass and oats. Lilias wrote about the joy of wild flowers — before pesticides had decimated their growth in the English hedgerows:

> All down the driftways, and in the odd corners of the headlands the midsummer flowers have bloomed in a ribbon of gay colours.
>
> Purple knapweed, brilliant rosie campion, creamy meadow-sweet, sky-blue chicory, the yellow agrimony (the poor man's tea of past days), rosebay and hawkweed, flaring ragwort, sombre spires of loosestrife, the delicate mauve pinks of scabious and hemp agrimony, and the drooping crimson cups of the poppies. Here and there, too, you would find the herbs whose virtues are almost forgotten; hound's-tongue and bugloss and comfrey, wild chamomile and tansy, the humble fleabane and the fragrant balm.[10]

It was these evocations of the countryside that meant so much to people during the long hardships, the terrible tensions, and recurring tragedies. Singapore fell to the Japanese army in February 1942 but in the Beccles and Bungay newspaper, the news of the prisoner-of-war status of the soldiers of the Norfolk Regiment on the infamous Burma railway only filtered back to their families during the long months of 1943.

Lilias infused her essays with a sense of solidarity and stability through local and personal history. One theme that was popular at the time was the stalwartness of yeoman farmers. The figure of the yeoman had an appealing robust Shakespearean style. She looked back to a letter written by her grandfather, Squire William Haggard of Bradenham, and his view of what English history and rural history was all about. He described the huge wealth that the wool trade brought to East Anglia, the open-field system and the commons, then in the wake of the Black Death and labour shortages, the shift to enclosures which created both an under class of disinherited workers but also eventually a new class of Yeoman farmers who flourished "and built hundreds of those small 'manors' ...

9   LRH *A Country Scrapbook*, 90.
10   Ibid, 116_177.

perfect examples of the best type of rural dwelling."[11]

The redoubtable figure of the yeoman farmer had been summoned up by Christopher Turnor, a Lincolnshire landowner, who proposed a vast increase in food production based on farms run by owner-occupiers — that is, yeoman farmers — and increased investment in farming via social credit. Turnor had visited both Italy and Germany to see how they were managing things and had been impressed by their achievements. He felt that a dislike for their fascist politics should not prevent a study of their methods. His book *Yeoman Calling* was published in 1939 — too late to be taken up as a policy but the ideas were in circulation.

Henry Williamson newly arrived at his Stiffkey farm. Courtesy of Anne Williamson

It was certainly the idea that Henry Williamson was working out in Stiffkey. It was he who suggested to Faber that Lilias' columns, edited, would make a good anthology and helped her pull together the first batch which would be called *Norfolk Life*. Fortunately for the less-than-methodical Lilias, Margaret had kept all the columns in scrapbooks which were duly sent off to Faber but the initial reaction was not positive.

On July 15th 1941 Lilias wrote to "Dear Mr Williamson":

> I quite see what Faber means, the difficulty has all along been
> very apparent to me but with the help of your suggestions I think
> it could be made into a book which would have enough "thread"
> through it to serve. I think I could do it all right, if anyone had
> seen the M.S. of *I Walked* and much more of *The Rabbit Skin Cap*,
> I do not think any publisher would have looked at it twice! I had
> to cut quite two thirds of the material of the latter.[12]

Even though it was early days, she wrote that she didn't care about the money since it would all go in income tax but what she wanted was to pave the way for a book about her father. It would be a means to an end. Her father was still her focus and when her cousin Godfrey, a diplomat in New York, came to visit she realised just how much her father had brought the public world into Ditchingham and, since his death, how relatively limited her life had become.

> The weeks which fly past with such breathless rapidity, and yet
> seem filled with a mass of unimportant details; the house and

11   Ibid, 125.
12   Letter in the Williamson Collection.

housekeeping ... blocked ditches, smoking chimneys, leaking
coppers, sagging gutters, and outworn farm premises. The hours
spent on cherishing chickens, filling in forms, dealing with
billeting papers, collecting savings — with lighter interludes of
making jam and bottling fruit. So much to do, and yet, when
looked at in the aggregate, so little done, or, like the nettles and
thistles upon which one wages incessant and backbreaking war,
no sooner done then all to do again.[13]

Nevertheless at Michaelmas, although she was saddened and distressed by the
events of the war, she took comfort in the harvest display at Ditchingham church:

I never remember summer and autumn gathered together in
such a blaze of colour within those old dim walls before. Flaming
dahlias and golden and red roses — all the fruits of our gardens,
scarlet and crimson apples, earth-hued potatoes, ruddy carrots,
dark globes of beet, green and orange marrows, the pale spheres
of eggs, grouped amidst the bending sheaves of corn. "Immortal
corn", as a friend of mine called it the other day, the eternal
symbol of man's necessity relying upon nature's miracle.[14]

Reflecting on the changing role of women in society Lilias wrote a long piece
about Mary Wollstonecraft:

I wonder how many have even heard of the first woman who
championed their freedom, and yet by a tragic twist of fate was
destined to remind them of the chink in their armour — their
womanhood.

Committed as she was to nurturing family life, Lilias understood only too well
the impossible pulls of different loyalties.[15]

By October 1941 Lilias and Margaret had met up with Henry Williamson.
Lilias was so alarmed by him that she had "cast myself on Pa Seago" for advice. Mr
Seago, Ted's father, assessed him as "one of those people with split personality
— one side gentle and loves animals etc and the other definitely sadistic
unconsciously". Lilias then realised that this "would account for all the trouble
with his [Henry's] wife and his mental upsets as it's one side warring against the
other all the time . . . I expect Loetitia is threatening divorce and probably some
pretty awful disclosures which accounts for his hints of scandal. I am not sure
that dear Henry is really quite what we thought him on mature reflection and
I am pretty sure he is a liar but perhaps more or less unconsciously." Lilias was

---

13 *A Country Scrapbook,* 126/7.
14 Ibid, 139.
15 Ibid, 151.

concerned enough to caution Margaret, "Anyhow be careful my dear while alone
and unprotected if he turns up on the doorstep as I expect he will!"[16]

Not surprisingly after the anxieties raised by this initial contact very little
progress was made on producing a collection of her journalism and Williamson,
having written notes for a foreword, approached her again in March of 1942. She
said that she had abandoned the *Eastern Daily Press* to start writing *The Lamp
of Memory* (presumably the working title for the biography of her father which
had long been in her mind) but promised to start again in April. She was happy
for him to take a look at her notebooks but insisted on paying for typing and
any other expenses. She mentioned that she had a bad cold, had been wrestling
200-year-old culverts blocked with hundredweights of soil brought down by frost
and rain and Bren gun carriers on top of the hill.

Lilias was adamant that the book should be slight and inexpensive — she wrote
to Henry:

> I do not mind in the least if I make a profit and as I told you do
> not ask for any advance royalty. One of the things which has
> pleased me most about all the letters I have had, is that many
> people who are ill or crippled seem to have found a great deal
> of pleasure in reading the Diary and later those articles which I
> have done since the war. In fact I think if your people do not in
> the end want it I shall try to arrange to bring it out locally and
> sell it through the EDP office.[17]

Given her concerns about his character, she might indeed have preferred
that option. She finished the letter by saying, "it's the hell of a life these days, no
time for anything," which indicated the pressure she was under. Kitty Carr had
succumbed to dropsy and all her livestock had to be cared for. In addition Lilias
was finding the care of her now bed-ridden mother too much to deal with and
Angie was resisting getting paid help. In a letter to Margaret Lilias wrote: "I am
not going to spend the rest of my days sitting in Mum's bedroom and I have said
so!!!"

In his introduction Williamson said that he never wrote for money himself
and didn't have the time to write about the north Norfolk coast while he was
trying to get the Stiffkey farm back into heart. This seems a little disingenuous
since he had been writing a column for the *Daily Express*. Moreover a letter to him
from Lilias suggests that he had been asking her about the possibility of writing
for the *Eastern Daily Press*. Lilias discussed possible *nom de plumes*, discouraging
him from choosing "Countryman" which was so close to her own by-line. She

---

[16]　　Letter in the Cheyne Collection.
[17]　　Undated letter from LRH to Henry Williamson, HW Estate collection.

warned that the *EDP* editors "hate anything involved or High Brow". She also revealed that long ago she had found another pseudonym for herself, "Susan Throstle" which she had spotted on a village shop near Newmarket. She had given "Susan Throstle" various attributes, such as singing in the village choir, and the name itself sounds like a bird song. This alter-ego "abominates lots of things that you think essential to the salvation of man!!"[18] Thus she dismissed Williamson's politics.

Williamson's introduction to *Norfolk Life* served the purpose of giving Lilias the benefit of his fame. Lilias was very grateful to him and acquiesced to his editing advice about the title. However, his criticism of her newspaper articles brought another sharp reaction from her about his politics. On September 23rd 1942 she wrote:

> As to your reproaches about propaganda you can tick me off anytime you like for being dull or careless or lacking style[,] judgement, anything you like as its not always easy as you know to write weekly articles of equal merit to order for years on end — and I'll thank you for it — because "I know my betters when I see them" but don't accuse me of propaganda for the sake of it! What I said I felt and meant. I think everyone of us who have young things whom they love ought to thank whatever gods they worship every day that as a country we have not had to endure what Europe is enduring. If what I said made even one person think a bit it wasn't wasted because heaven knows they don't — in the village anyhow. I think myself if we had understood the vast indifference of this country and the value of right propaganda England would not be where she is now. It's too late I know and we probably differ materially as to what is the right propaganda.[19]

She did not withdraw her friendship but her letters to him are very downright and frank, much more so than those to her family and Margaret.

In another undated letter written towards the end of 1942 Lilias commiserated with Henry about his having to get rid of his unprofitable cows but suggesting his talents were with land and machines. She pointed out that livestock and vegetables need affection: "this isn't merely middle aged sentiment. I've lived with animals and kept them all my life and seen it over and over again." Evidently she felt that Williamson was short on empathy. She also added that she was glad he was keeping a "guarded tongue" because "The reverse can hardly do any

18   Undated letter from LRH to Henry Williamson, HW Estate collection.
19   Letter from LRH to Henry Williamson September 23rd – HW Estate collection.

good just now" although she added, semi-humorously, that she was a fine one to be giving this advice since she was most "unguarded in her utterances". Her postscript gives the letter its approximate time: "I am giving up the articles in the EDP at Xmas as I must get on with the book and do a little concentration." As well as her father's biography she also had a new idea to write about a legendary seventeenth century character, Ned Baldry, and his horse Old Shell — "all horsey and ye old countryside!!" Meanwhile she looked around at the autumn scenes:

> This week I went with a friend on business bent for a day out in the car, the sort of expedition the joys of which are almost forgotten. Going through Norwich, where every turn shows some tragic scene of broken and roofless homes and shattered buildings, I thought we must be thankful that bombing, even severe bombing, cannot be compared with heavy shelling for destruction. I do not think anyone could ever forget the ruins of some of the Belgian towns after the first world war, surrounded by twisted, shell-torn tracks which had once been roads, and a countryside blasted, barren, and utterly desolate. Unlike Europe, from this we have so far been saved. The heart of England stands as it did, almost unscathed.
>
> Late as the season is, the last remnants of the bitter weeks behind us are finally wiped out, and summer has clothed the world in the brilliance of fields golden with buttercups, hedges foaming like a white sea with blossom, and the depths of the beech woods lost in a lavender mist of bluebells.[20]

In the New Year of 1943 she wrote again to Williamson saying that her last domestic help had left and she had many letters to answer from readers. The manuscript for *Norfolk Life* had come back at 65,000 words and she would be writing the additional links. She said she wasn't worried if Henry was unable to bring off the publishing with Faber. She knew that the publishing world was in a "stew"[21] but she was getting many letters from people who could not get hold of copies of *I Walked by Night* and *The Rabbit Skin Cap* and second-hand booksellers were advertising for them. A friend had been working on the typing of *Norfolk Life* and with family troubles had had a difficult time getting it done. At Ditchingham they had welcomed three American Officers to Christmas lunch who had pitched in willingly with the family. "This blasted snow" added to the "joys of Life" she wrote flippantly; Ted Seago had sent a copy of his new book for Christmas.

20   LRH, *Country Scrapbook*, 177.
21   This would have been because of severe paper shortages that affected all writers.

An article in the January 2nd 1943 edition of the *EDP* informed its readers that artificial fertilizers were "good farming". Some farmers were reluctant to use their allocation of phosphate and potash but the newspaper tried to reassure them. The Ministry of Agriculture wanted all gardens turned over to vegetable production and for as many women and children as possible to help cultivate the allotments and to aim for self-sufficiency among local institutions, schools and industry. Beccles alone had sixty acres of allotments.[22]

In a letter of February 2nd 1943 Lilias wrote to Henry apologising for not having written since the return of the manuscript. She had been struggling with a representative of the Ministry of Supply over the Bath House road and the government timber carting. She had received a letter from Mr De la Mare of Faber who seemed pleased with the manuscript and had written to Henry about the agreement. Lilias again emphasised her gratitude. She had hoped to come over for a visit with Margaret on the previous weekend but her dog, Dido, was heavily pregnant and had in fact produced seven puppies on the Saturday. They were unfortunately all black — which had disappointed "Pa Seago" who had wanted a yellow one. They had had severe gales and floods in Ditchingham and the farm "is a swamp and depressing to look at".

In March 1943 Lilias' brilliant, handsome and charismatic nephew, Stephen Haggard, died from a gunshot wound on a train in Palestine.

Stephen Haggard.
Courtesy Piers Haggard.

Lilias wrote to Margaret:

Poor Godfrey — both sons and a grandson gone already. I am afraid he will be desperately upset. It has been a most depressing week.[23]

Stephen's fame as a stage and film actor, a poet and, most recently, as a novelist had been emerging before the war started. He had written a story called *Nya* with a theme that prefigured Nabokov's *Lolita*. Stephen's charm and talent were recorded by Christopher Hassall in *The Timeless Quest* (1948). One of his two sisters, Virginia, who also determined on an artist's life, recorded in her book *Lifeline* that the coroner's verdict on his death was

---

[22] Beccles and Bungay newspaper January 30th 1943.
[23] Letter in the Cheyne Collection. March 4th 1943.

suicide.[24] Stephen had a strain of volatility in his nature that the Haggards put down to their Amyand antecedents and he had been in despair over a new love affair.

In the spring of 1943 Churchill rescinded the prohibition on ringing church bells on Sundays and special occasions. Lilias was quick to pick up the implication and to enhance its significance through a narrative of collective history:

> Brazen, barbaric and archaic survivals of an older world they
> may be, but something in their deep vibrating harmonies is apt
> to reach down into the heart of man and quicken to life many
> things not dead but sleeping.[25]

In June the proofs arrived but no let up on the wartime demands on civilians. Lilias wrote to Henry:

> What are we to do about these 'ere proofs! I am completely stuck
> here as I am wrestling with a Wings for Victory[26] week. I think I
> had better correct mine and let you have it. There does not as a
> matter of fact seem much to correct but perhaps your expert eye
> will find some more as I have not the MS[,] Margaret has got
> them all.
>
> I think your first chapter is now excellent. No I didn't take any
> offence about the Victorian flavours. I belong firmly to that era!
>
> M and I are completely divorced from Hilldrop[27] [Margaret's
> cottage at Wiveton] at the moment as her sister is away in
> Ireland for a month and she has to be at home with Mama. She
> also for her sins has a Wings for Victory week beginning today.
>   …
>
> I hope all goes well with you as it does here except I have had
> a slight breeze as chairman of the village charity trust lands and
> came near to walking out of a meeting after a violent passage of
> arms with our local "Bolshie" farmer! Very funny really but I fear
> not v. dignified. I was in a rage and so was he!
>
> Yours LRH[28]

24   *Lifeline* (Milton Keynes, UK; Authorhouse;2009). His son Piers Haggard
      became a successful film director.
25   LRH, *Country Scrapbook*, 217.
26   This dates the letter to circa 5ᵗʰ June 1943 when Beccles and Bungay had their
      Wings for Victory fund-raising week.
27   They had given it the same name as Rider and Cochrane's house in Newcastle,
      Natal.
28   Letter from LRH to Henry Williamson, HW Estate collection

A few days later, in a letter of June 7th 1943, she again discussed the correction of proofs. Henry had been in hospital with appendicitis and Lilias was expecting both her youngest nephew (Mark) back on leave from two years in the Mediterranean with the Navy and a young cousin on sick leave with lung trouble who had asked if he could be "fed up and looked after". Ditchingham continued to be the "lost dogs' home" of the Haggard family only now it was Lilias who looked after them all. Lilias was hoping to get up to stay with Margaret at Wiveton and if so would visit Henry along the coast. In July 1943 Lilias wrote again having heard via the *Eastern Daily Press* that Henry was out of hospital. She had seen Ted Seago recently and he was looking well and she thought his new book would do well but the death of his friend Bernard Clegg "has rather spoilt the pleasure in the whole thing".

By the autumn the war was starting to swing towards the Allies. The British army was driving north through Italy. Henry Williamson was writing weekly articles for the EDP about his farming under the banner "Green Fields and Pavements".

Norfolk Life was published early in the autumn of 1943; it was reviewed by all the major national papers including *The Spectator*, *The Listener*, *Country Life*, *Punch* and *The Sunday Times*. The reviewer for *The Times Literary Supplement* noticed that it was the personality behind the diary entries that was so attractive. A. C. Boyd for *Books of the Month* applauded the "delicate and sensitive evocation of country sights and sounds" but also noticed that Lilias portrayed "a landscape without figures".

The first print-run of 5000 copies was over-subscribed and Faber had to print another 2000 at once and then realised it would not be enough. The book rapidly went into eight impressions.[29] Although Williamson had been the initiator and conduit, his footnotes are, if anything, a distraction and jar with Lilias' style. It is her book. Adrian Bell commented in his review that the quality of the book lay in the writer's personality which lent such a happy note to the day-to-day happenings in garden and village. He claimed that Miss Rider Haggard was more than a country diarist, she was a "trustee . . . of that essential England which must emerge intact from war and industrialism if England herself is to survive and lead the world back to sanity".

Lady Haggard died on September 4th 1943. Lilias described the emptiness in the house when she wrote to Margaret. She felt that "all the old life is gone for good". Lilias had been with her when she died and found the experience "pretty shattering". The ensuing weeks were also pretty shattering with rows about the inheritance and where everyone was to live. Dolly had cancer of the womb and was due to go into hospital. Angie had dreadful nerves and no one knew how they

---

[29]   Letter from Faber and Faber to LRH October 12th 1943, in the Cheyne Collection.

were going to manage financially. The elderly Hildyard sisters, who had helped raise Lilias, had come to stay and were another burden on the household; they had no concept of rationing. Lilias was trying to find a maid or household help but it was almost impossible in wartime and as she said candidly : " If I found a family like this I should run a mile." By October she was ill herself and realised they would have to break up the house and put most of their parents' possessions up for auction. There would be very little left in terms of cash and they would all have to tighten their belts.

Lady Haggard left the whole estate to Angie but there was no question of anyone having to leave. All three sisters began a grand clear out of Ditchingham House with a view to letting it. Furniture and personal possessions of four generations of Haggards and Margitsons went into a two-day sale. In order to erase the indiscretions of their forebears many family papers were burnt.

By now people in public life were giving a good deal of thought to post-war reconstruction. In October 1943 there had been a Town and Country Planning Conference presided over by W. S. Morrison, the minister for Town and Country Planning.[30] In response to an article in the national press the EDP argued that the practice of agriculture was entirely compatible with the preservation of rural beauty. The travesties of agri-business had yet to make themselves known. Late in the month, on the October 27th, the Earl of Portsmouth made his maiden speech in the House of Lords on the subject of the impoverishment of the soil by artificial fertilizers which would eventually lead to ill-health and disease in humans and animals. In reply the Duke of Norfolk said that those who decried fertilisers were doing a disservice to the farmer and the country.

With the high demand for copies there had been distribution problems with *Norfolk Life* so that Lilias had been buying copies herself from Faber to supply shops in Bungay. "What a hopeless mess Jarrolds have made of it", she moaned to Margaret.[31] The family were awaiting probate and didn't know yet what they would be doing with Ditchingham House.

In researching her biography of her father Lilias did not have to go far for the material; everything concerning his life from 1900 to 1926 had been kept but initially she could not find anything earlier. Rider's own two volume autobiography, *The Days of My Life*, which had been published after his death in 1926, drew on his older letters and notes must be in the house somewhere. She and Angie together matched up clues and keys and eventually found a locked iron box in the basement containing the treasure trove of earlier family letters, particularly Rider's letters from Africa before and after his marriage.

[30]   W .S. Morrison, (1893-1961) later 1st Viscount Dunrossil.
[31]   Whether Jarrolds were acting as retailers or distributers is not clear. Latimer Trend & Co, Plymouth, were the printers.

By April 1944 she had resumed writing for the EDP — only once a month but in a better slot on the first Saturday. Much of her subject matter was about birds — their habits and behaviours — of which she was a keen observer. Her focus and concentration are notable. From these monthly articles we also learn that Abbott Smith (the Fairbridge Farm boy from Rhodesia) had joined the US Navy and stopped at Ditchingham on his way to Europe in 1944. "Margaret and I" painted the scullery and Lilias, ever clumsy, spilled the paint all over the floor. Margaret was planting out in the garden when bombers flew over. By summer the Americans were liberating France but Lilias was still writing about wildlife — rabbits, stoats and chickens. Margaret at last learned to milk the cow. Lilias, who we hear looked a bit like a tramp when she was home, wearing an ancient Burberry several sizes too large, a nephew's rubber boots, and a faded green beret, got up one morning, spotted a rabbit from the bathroom and quickly took up her shotgun and fired from the window. Margaret was rather critical of the fact that her gun had been ready-loaded for which Lilias seems a little shame-faced, but no less triumphant for having dispatched the rabbit. Grebes and ducks were the subject of her September piece. Abbott, back on leave, filled them in with what was happening in Europe: the Germans were destroying everything they could in their retreat but generally left mirrors intact — an odd superstition under the circumstances.

With the Americans entering the war and air bases springing up all over East Anglia there was a new novelty on the Home Front — black Americans were evident in the villages and country towns where foreigners of any kind were a rarity. Lilias took the opportunity to discourse on slavery:

> Some coloured [sic] troops in the district gave a recital after
> morning service in our church, I suppose the first time the old
> walls have echoed to those lovely but alien voices. The deep
> harmonies and organ-like resonance, unknown in any white
> man, echo the underlying tragedy and all the immense sorrows of
> their race.[32]

The last surviving letter from Lilias to Henry Williamson is dated December 5th 1944.[33] She had been busy with proofs for a reprint of *I Walked By Night* and apologised for her lateness in replying. Williamson had evidently offered to help her with any further collection of articles but she forthrightly declined:

> …honestly Henry I have had such a drubbing both from friends

[32]   LRH, *A Country Scrapbook*, 224.
[33]   There are two from him to Margaret in 1946 when he was back in Devon on
       his own. Lilias remained friends with Loetitia who came to live in Bungay.
       Margaret left a substantial legacy to one of her daughters.

and strangers about that editing of *Norfolk Life* that never again will I allow anyone to touch a book of mine. Good or bad they have got to stand on their own legs. Ever so many thanks all the same for the offer.

She had made her position quite plain.

10

Home-Grown Harvest

In April 1945 Julian Tennyson, the young writer who had visited Lilias in 1938, died in Burma. He had written to her quite recently saying that after three and half years away he was looking forward to returning to Peasenhall and his beloved Suffolk countryside. His death jarred Lilias' heart as so many others over the past few years had done.

When the war in Europe finished in May Lilias advocated a close relationship to the land and country life as the wholesome way forward for the battered soul of the country. She mused on what was really the "heart's desire" and thought it was to do with the simple joys of home and hearth. She was glad to be able to move back to the Bath House and took deep solace in its isolated position finding company in the elemental energy of the river. The water and the wildlife spoke to her, perhaps at some archaic level, and deeply satisfied her; she was never lonely with nature.

In the post-war period both domesticity and close observation became matters of national preoccupation. New housing and new planning for a family life were priorities while observation was a habit encouraged by a variety of initiatives intent on democratising the ability to appreciate nature, landscape, wildlife, architecture and English history.[1] This was a period of new enthusiasm for guides to birdlife and wild life, Shell guides, and the work of local and landscape historian W. G. Hoskins and English architectural historian John Betjeman.

Faber published Lilias' second collection of essays called *Norfolk Notebook* just after the war. Adrian Bell reviewed it for *The Times Literary Supplement* and remarked on her sincerity which he defined as "a habit of equipoise" in a world of suffering of which she was deeply aware. *The Spectator* noted that as with all good journals it was a portrait of its author — "in this case an English country woman of rare personality, wise, humorous, and practical, a woman in whom fact and imagination are nicely mated".

---

[1]   *Landscape and Englishness* Chapter 7, "Citizens in Reconstruction".

At the beginning of 1946 she began a new series of fortnightly "Countrywoman" columns for the EDP but by the end of the year she was ready to continue the serious work of writing her father's biography. She positioned herself in her father's old study with the wide casement windows looking out across the back garden and towards the river valley. This was her journey towards the man who had commanded her life, not just in himself as the father she adored, but in the paternal authority that surrounded her at Ditchingham. Yet it was an authority challenged both by the fact that the estate was her mother's inheritance and by Rider's own struggle with "She" — in Jungian terms, his *anima*. And where was Lilias in this riddle of nature and culture? Perhaps she hoped to find out or perhaps she simply could not escape him; one way or the other the book was essentially her life's work.

After leaving school at sixteen, Nada pursued her interest in dancing — classical, historical and modern. In this she had been influenced and encouraged by Phoebe Haggard, daughter of Jack Haggard. Nada studied at a residential college in Leicestershire and, after graduating, she taught there and at other schools on a day basis. During 1947 Nada Haggard, aged twenty-two, married

Wedding party outside Ditchingham church: Lilias second from right, Mark Cheyne far left.
Cheyne Collection.

her cousin Mark Cheyne, nine years her senior, whom she had known all her life. This marriage had in it the potential for solving the future of the estate. More immediately Nada became a naval wife including periods stationed in Malta.[2]

In Norwich there was a new young woman's editor at the *Eastern Daily Press*, Jean Goodman.[3] When Lilias resumed her articles in a January 1948 column she responded to a letter that H. J. Massingham had written to the *Times Literary Supplement* about "timeless principles". She set out her belief unequivocally:

> Apparently, it does not occur to many of those who cry "Progress" that there are certain fundamental laws which govern men and nature upon which the contentment and proper balance of mind and body must be built. The meaning of "nostalgia" is "return journey" or "return home". It looks as if there are many things to which (if we are to Progress) we must return, if we would find a way to restore order, harmony and happiness, amidst the scientific bedlam we have created.

Although Lilias did not express herself in the terms that environmentalists would do later, she does capture the essence of their message. Her words prefigure those of New Age writers such as Miriam Simos in *The Spiral Dance*:

> . . . "we must return to the circle". The circle is the ecological circle, the circle of the interdependence of all living organisms. Civilization must return to harmony with nature.[4]

Lilias' holistic view was well ahead of the nature movement of the time which was constructing reservations and conservation areas — managed ecology — as evidenced at Minsmere Level in Suffolk and at Wheatfen in Norfolk. The latter was created by the naturalist Ted Ellis, known to both Lilias and Margaret.

Just as she had visited the battlefields of France after WWI, in 1949 Lilias and her friend Henta Scudamore took a boat trip down the Rhine. They saw the devastation of the Allied bombing raids in Cologne, Coblenz, Mainz, Worms and Mannheim. Writing to suit the EDP she commented on the landscape, the vineyards, the municipal planting of flowers and the sense of continuity with an old Germany through a Wine Feast in Koenigswinter. It was anodyne stuff but readable. Privately she wrote to Margaret:

> . . . it is not a case of bomb damage in the sense as we

---

2   Miss Brown had been Mark's governess before he went to boarding school, so, as well as both being raised at Ditchingham, the two children would have had a very similar upbringing.

3   Jean Goodman later wrote the biography *Edward Seago: A Wider Canvas*, (Banham, Erskine Press, 2002).

4   Quoted in *The Penguin Book of New Age and Holistic Writing*, 219.

understand it but complete obliteration. As to Cologne it is
quite indescribable, all those lovely bridges gone as they are
everywhere blown up by the Germans in the retreat.[5]

Lilias had been a Parish Councillor since the early 1930s and in 1949 she
decided to stand as an Independent candidate for Norfolk County Council which
in those days met at the Shire Hall, near the Castle, in Norwich. She was elected
in April and amongst her colleagues were Lt. Col. B. M. Edwards (chairman),
Sir Henry Upcher, Mr A. Cozens-Hardy, Sir Bartle Frere, Lady Walsingham, the
Earl of Albermarle, Major Astley, Sir Edward Preston Bt and representatives of
the Barclay, Gaymer and Bullard families. These were the pillars – and the elite
– of the county, the people who ran Norfolk. The committees she sat on were
the Printing Committee, Education, Wild Birds Protection Act, Smallholdings
and Youth Employment Service for South-East Norfolk.[6] She served her two-
year term and was then succeeded by William George Clark of Loddon Road,
Ditchingham.

After Lady Haggard's death and a period of clearance, Ditchingham House
was let to tenants who ran it as a guest house. At some time in this period Angie
and Dolly shared a house, "Battlecrease", that had once belonged to Julia (Bazett's
widow) on the outskirts of London.

In 1949 or early in 1950 a young woman named Margaret Sawbridge came
to work for Lilias to type up the manuscript of Rider's biography, now called
The Cloak that I Left. Margaret's father, who was the rector of Newton Flotman,
had met Lilias on committees,[7] and Margaret herself had been at St Felix School
where, although she was several years older, she had known Nada slightly.

Margaret, as a vicar's daughter, was not part of the county social set. Her father
had been a widower with five children and her mother, his second wife, had been
their nanny so there was, for those times, a significant social gap. Margaret
noticed that Lilias would never come into her home when she dropped her off by
car and she felt this was because she did not find her mother socially acceptable –
which was quite likely since Lilias herself admitted in a letter to Margaret that she
could be "stuffy" and often mentioned people's acceptability or unacceptability
in terms of class.

With Margaret Spurrell so often at the Bath House it was not convenient
to have two "Margarets" so Lilias always called Margaret Sawbridge "Peggy"
– a childhood nickname that she had been trying to outgrow. However, as an
employer Lilias seems to have been easy-going although we don't know how

5   Letter from LRH to MS 25 September 1949, Cheyne Collection.
6   Norfolk County Council Proceedings, NRO.
7   Possibly the Norfolk Small Industries Committee.

much she paid. Peggy would work in the mornings but after lunch Lilias would encourage walks or she would row downstream after tea. If it was a very fine morning Lilias would suggest a break even in the morning and ask Peggy to fetch milk from a white farm house across the Bungay Road. Sometimes Kitty Athill who was living in the next house along the valley from

Bath House interior: Lilias in her drawing room.
Cheyne Collection.

the Bath House would give her a lift in her pony and trap. In the evenings Peggy would type business letters for Lilias on her own typewriter set up on a card table in her bedroom.

Peggy Sawbridge did not actively dislike Lilias but she found her very irritating partly because she was totally absorbed in her dogs. Peggy remembered a walk on Outney Common when she tried several times to attract Lilias' attention to a stunning sunset but Lilias just kept on talking to her dogs. However, when she did try to help Peggy, who was an aspiring writer herself, the tuition was not welcomed.

Lilias' second cousin Jill Tucker and her husband were living in a cottage on the estate.[8] He had been damaged by the war and was learning to grow vegetables and Peggy Sawbridge recalled that Lilias was privately rather scathing about him. Lilias asked Jill Tucker to advise Peggy on where to buy clothes but did not take into account that Henry Ashe on London Street and Brahams on the Back-of-the-Inns were well beyond Peggy's pocket. Lilias herself was not fashionably dressed but wore old and seated tweeds — but no doubt expensive when first bought. Lilias also had a habit of wearing hats at lunch and a beret at tea time.

Lilias tried to match-make by leaving Peggy rather obviously alone with one of her visitors — a young man whom Peggy recalled was Michael Boardman (a son of the Norwich architect, Edward Boardman). Neither she nor Michael was interested in each other romantically but they had a friendly chat.

If Peggy Sawbridge was not enthusiastic about her employer, Lilias' view of Peggy was equally unflattering. In a letter to Margaret she mentions that she was taking Peggy to lunch at Kirby Cane Hall with the Crisp family and that "I warned

---

8   Ella Geraldine Maddison-Green, a grand-daughter of Ella Haggard, Rider's eldest sister married to Lt-Col Harvey Domvile Tucker.

them that Peggy was a bit dumb but they didn't seem to mind at all."[9] Despite both their reservations, the working arrangement lasted on and off for a number of years.

The third collection of Lilias' essays, *A Country Scrapbook* (Faber & Faber 1950), is a mature work: the essays are more composed, more emotionally adventurous and this development was favourably reviewed. It was published in October 1950 and the November 3rd edition of *Country Life* said that it exhibited "that deep instinctive love of country life that we have come to expect from her". The reviewer felt that although the book covered the war years, Norfolk in war-time was incidental to the timeless aspects of country life. After one or two quibbles he exclaimed "But how well she writes!" *The Times Literary Supplement* took a different slant saying that "the war is felt rather as an imminent shadow. The country silence takes on a listening tension; at any moment the enemy may come floating out of the sky as harmless-looking as thistledown." Again Lilias' personality was noted and the fact that in her life "action and meditation implement and do not confound each other". The following year Lilias was one of the personalities at the Jarrold's Book Fair standing alongside R. H. Mottram in the press photographs.

The Cloak that I Left was published in 1951 by Hodder and Stoughton. The amount of first-hand detail has made it a source book for all the biographies that have followed. It is an affectionate rather than a critical biography and while it is not an untruthful book there is a considerable degree of discretion. Lilias brought some of the family secrets out but not exactly into the open; they are sometimes carefully camouflaged. Her cousin Harry wrote to her:

> You size up our uncles with consummate tact, but very justly
> and I feel your power of restraint must have been severely taxed.
> They certainly were a rum lot and good fellows as they were,
> their words and deeds, when in company, used to make me blush
> — always a weakness of mine when I was a sensitive youngster.[10]

Lilias explored fairly thoroughly Rider's love for Lilly Jackson although she gives her the name "Lilith".[11] She did not reveal the full, dreadful, story of Lilly Jackson's marriage — perhaps because Lilly's sons were still living.[12] Nor did Lilias reveal that Rider was in dire financial straits when he proposed to the heiress Louisa Margitson.

9   Letter from LRH to Margaret Spurrell 1953, Cheyne Collection.
10   Letter from Hugh Vernon Haggard to LRH July 10th 1951. Cheyne Collection.
11   One derivation is from Isaiah 34:14 and seems to imply a female demon.
     In Jewish folklore Lilith was Adam's first wife who refused to become
     subservient to him.
12   She did leave enough clues for D. S. Higgins to discover Lilly's identity while
     researching his 1981 biography *Rider Haggard: The Great Storyteller*.

As he matured he looked back with a stricken conscience at his irresponsible, but love-struck, behaviour. After he became successful he wrote to Louie:

> I cannot tell you my dear what a pleasure it will be to me to find myself in a position to give you back the home again which in a way you lost by marrying me . . . relieved my conscience of a great weight.
>
> I do not think I had any business to marry you when I did — it was pulling you down in the world.[13]

Lilias rather glosses over the fact that Rider's brother Andrew had already proposed to Louie and been rejected; Andrew was certainly looking for a rich wife for as an army officer he had very poor prospects and had already made one unwise marriage which he kept secret, and later married for money into a family which, understandably, resented him. Fortunately Louie, young though she was, had been a good judge of character.

Admiral Hugh Vernon Haggard, probably his wife Dorothy and Lilias at the Bath House. Cheyne Collection.

Most tellingly Lilias does not reveal explicitly that Rider had fathered a child in Africa. By euphemistically writing that "the accursed Amyand blood" was having its fling, the inevitable feminine complications ensued . . ."[14] she does imply an involvement and later she referred to a "sin" he had committed in his youth; it was for later biographers to explore the details.[15] Rider and Arthur Cochrane both had sexual adventures in Africa with white settlers. Rider's child was born to a married woman while Rider was in England and died soon after birth. Cochrane's letters informing him of the events have survived. Rider suffered terrible guilt from this and when his legitimate child died it was this old "sin" that preyed on his mind. He believed it

13 LRH, *The Cloak that I Left*, 133.
14 Ibid, 85. The Amyand blood is a reference to their Huguenot ancestors.
15 See *Diary of an African Journey* edited by Stephen Coan (Pietermaritzburg: University of Natal Press; 2000) and *Children of the Empire*.

was some kind of personal punishment. His morose grief and his repression of Jock's memory impacted on his whole family.

Lilias glossed over the rackety life he and Cochrane were living in the house that they ironically named "Palatial". Cochrane was sexually involved with a girl whom he was trying to avoid marrying. It was as a result of the trouble in which they found themselves that Rider and Cochrane moved from Rooi Point to the house called Hilldrop to try their hand at ostrich farming.

Lilias was not above white-washing her uncles either when she wrote that they were "unwaveringly faithful husbands".[16] In fact it seems to have been well-known in the family that the Squire was father to at least one known illegitimate child, Alfred Thacker, and quite possibly others at Bradenham. Maidservants were often seduced by their employers — and by sons as well as the father. William (Will) had a disastrous first marriage that ended in acrimonious divorce. Jack took his maid/mistress out to Noumea; he also had a common law wife and a whole second family in Portsmouth. Andrew hid his first marriage to a woman of a lower class whom he could never have introduced into his social circle; fortunately, from his point of view, she died young. He was very amorous and had a daughter whom it is hard to place. It was heavily hinted in letters that Alfred, whose wife was an invalid, sought solace elsewhere possibly with prostitutes. For all we know this was the tip of the iceberg. These extramarital relationships of varying kinds were tolerated if not approved in a straight-laced society in which the only legitimate outlet for sexuality was marriage. Much more shocking to our modern sensibilities is the fate of Cissie, one of Rider's three sisters, who was sent to an asylum and one strongly suspects that a contributory factor to her "madness" was being a sexual woman in a patriarchal society.[17]

Lilias said that Rider and Louie no longer had sex after she was born; he would have been, at thirty-six, far from middle-aged. He was often away from home for long periods but he was rather scared of women and liked his romantic fantasies. Godfrey said that he did not have a good manner with women unless they stood up to him — then he argued with them most enjoyably.

Lilias was evidently aware of public criticism of Rider's imperialism and said that its roots were in the period when he and Louie first went out to Africa with high hopes of making a new life for themselves as settlers.

> It was these months at Hilldrop that sowed in Rider the
> passionate sense of Imperial responsibilities which influenced
> so much of his after life. To the spirit of Imperialism, so often
> abused and misunderstood, he gave freely of all he had, serving

16   Ibid, 166.
17   See *Children of the Empire: the Victorian Haggards*.

its cause whole-heartedly and often infinitely to his own disadvantage.

This question of Rider's devout imperialism is important because it has ruined his appeal and his reputation for post 1960s generations. D. S. Higgins, who was a critical biographer, thought that:

> . . . Haggard saw himself as a protector of his race and culture.
> . . . He was not, however, an extremist urging the supremacy of a white Anglo-Saxon master-race. His enthusiastic advocacy of settlement in the Dominions was derived not from notions of racial conquest but from his informed sympathy for the appalling conditions in which lived his country's urban poor. [18]

Rider's Imperialism was a nationalistic reaction to the Boers, not to the indigenous peoples of Africa whose cultures fascinated him. Rider was never afraid of hard practical work and turned his hand to brick-making and hay-making, taking great pride in his labour and his profit. The Boers were amazed to see a white man rolling up his sleeves and not using "Kaffir" labour. The months spent at Hilldrop were in a historically critical period for British imperial policy in Africa when for the first time Britain was seen to be vulnerable. Rider himself had been part of the deputation which annexed the Transvaal in an attempt to bring the Boers under imperial law which would stop the Boers' near enslavement of the indigenous peoples. Rider believed in the integrity of his then chief Sir Theophilus Shepstone, an old Africa-hand, although Thomas Pakenham in *The Scramble for Africa* is less certain about his motives.[19]

Rider was still in the Transvaal during the legendary defeat of the British army at Isandlwana and its aftermath at Rorke's Drift. He heard news of it from a Hottentot woman some twenty hours before official news arrived via a messenger on horseback; an example of the shamanic powers which fascinated him. These battles led to the exit of Disraeli from Number 10 and Gladstone's return to power with a new Liberal policy of reversing the Annexation of the Transvaal — but not necessarily to self-rule. By the time the British took revenge at the battle of Ulundi, Rider was in England.

When Rider and Louie returned to Africa the various Boer factions had united in their demand for independence of the Transvaal. It could not have been a worse time; the British troops were headquartered at Newcastle very close to Hilldrop. Sir Garnet Wolseley, recently Governor of Natal, had left for India and

---

[18]   D. S. Higgins, *Rider Haggard The Great Storyteller*, 191.
[19]   Thomas Pakenham, *The Scramble for Africa* (London: 1991, Weidenfeld & Nicolson, 1991) 51 and 52.

been replaced by his protégée Sir George Colley.[20] Fatally, neither of them rated the Boers very highly as people or as soldiers and didn't think they would fight.

But fight they did. First in a series of raids and then at Majuba Hill on February 27th 1881 when they inflicted a humiliating defeat which was in part down to Colley's poor leadership, part the lack of preparation of the British troops and part down to the Boers' exceptional skill as riflemen while on the move. When his troops and his officers fled Colley did the "right" thing, he strode out into the open with a revolver in his hand and was shot through the forehead.

It was a huge insult to the British army to be defeated by a bunch of farmers, most of them teenagers. That Gladstone then made peace with the Boers thus betraying the British settlers was something that Rider found hard if not impossible to forgive. He and Louie planned to start again in Victoria Island, British Columbia, but that never happened. Gladstone's Liberal policy ruined Natal and the results were devastating both for the British and the natives. Why did Rider let that youthful humiliation colour his public life to such a deep hue of imperialism? It was partly because he was not a party man and could not engage successfully in political life, yet he did want a public career. It may also have been a result of his mother's background in India where her family had been so much part of the Raj and so affronted by the Mutiny. Empire was so much interwoven with his family life that not to uphold it seemed unimaginable.

Lilias asked her cousin Godfrey, the diplomat, to write an introduction to her biography; he gave his own memories of staying at Ditchingham and the atmosphere in the family circle. Godfrey's father, Alfred, disparaged Rider and called family life at Ditchingham "a mutual admiration society", which is certainly supported by the tone of Lilias' book, but there was also jealousy in Alfred's attitude; Godfrey came to love his uncle and was impressed by Rider's love of the land, his feeling of stewardship, and his dynastic sensibility which was thwarted by lack of a son. Godfrey could not fathom the feeling between Rider and Louie — whether he blamed her, or she blamed herself for the boy's death; or indeed whether he blamed her that Lilias was not a boy. So little was ever spoken about emotional matters but they must have observed each other closely over the years. The talk at the dining table was all facts, anecdotes and opinions delivered in a forthright manner. It was Godfrey, not Lilias, who revealed that Rider had a speech impediment and couldn't say Rs or Ws; according to Godfrey his family was unaware of the disability. It would have been rare in those days to have questioned what kind of sensitivity or trauma in a child might have led to the obstruction.

[20]   Colley had been secretary to the Viceroy of India, Lord Lytton, who was related both to Sir Henry Bulwer who had taken Rider to Africa, and Edward Bulwer-Lytton the novelist. The Bulwers of Heydon were a Norfolk family.

After the book was published Godfrey's aunt Aggie, Jack's widow, gave him a dressing-down for his representation of Louie as an impassive partner. This was not the case; she was proud and independent. The final point that Godfrey made dramatically was that Rider believed in reincarnation; reincarnation is not part of Christian theology, it is part of Eastern and primitive religions.

There are other examples of daughters writing biographies of their fathers. A. G. Street was a country writer, also in the de la Mare/Faber stable and also known to Williamson and others writing in the genre. His daughter wrote a memoir albeit in 1970 — twenty years later. Nevertheless it is noticeable that Mary remembered her father not only for his writing and broadcasting career but in relation to her own life — how he influenced her, what they shared. By contrast Lilias got up close, even inside Rider and when she mentions herself it is in the third person and only when it was relevant to him.

The Cloak that I Left is without doubt a "father's daughter's" book but what exactly does that mean? Jungian psychoanalyst Marion Woodman has written about this particular pattern of female psychology in *The Pregnant Virgin*.[21] It is her view that women who bond with their father are in one sense abandoned — that is, banned from relationships with other men and from creating their own children — but in another sense have a quest for their own inner story and are compelled into a relationship with their own creative imagination. They have fathers who have a boyish, immature psychology and ambivalent attitudes to women; on the one hand they are deeply attached to their mothers, as Rider was, on the other hand they resent their own vulnerability to women and are intent on "destroying any witch that would seduce him into her power". Critic Stephen Arata argues in his book *Fictions of Loss* that Rider recognised his mother as the source of his creativity but resented her suffocating influence; his mother's name, Ella, is Spanish for "She".[22] There are many examples of the death of witches in Rider's stories — his second book was called *The Witch's Head* and Ayesha dies as a decaying crone. Woodman is unequivocal as to the possible effect on such a man's daughter if his relationship with his wife (who is quite likely to be uncomfortable with her own body and bodily functions) founders and the daughter cannot bond with her:

> The child is trapped in spiritual incest, even more dangerous than actual incest because neither he nor she has any reason to suspect that something is amiss.
>
> . . .
>
> The puer's [boyish man's] shadow … may murder not only witches but the femininity of his little daughter as well.

21   Marion Woodman *The Pregnant Virgin*, (Toronto: Inner City Books, 1985)..
22   *Fictions of Loss in the Victorian Fin de Siècle*, 103.

The Cloak that I Left was published in 1951 at the same time as the opening of the Festival of Britain which was staged to say good-bye to austerity and usher in a new Elizabethan age. Even so the name of Rider Haggard still attracted interest — helped by the fact that a new film of *King Solomon's Mines* starring Stewart Granger had been released in 1950. The May 26th 1951 edition of *The Illustrated London News* gave a full page feature on Lilias' biography which was really a summary of Rider's life. Many reviews were simply appreciative notices but it was not all plain sailing. R.G. Pine in *Punch* complained that the book was written in a "tone of exalted filial piety" and "throws little light on the psychological origins or value of his [Rider's] work". Pine found the portrait of Rider "unintentionally repellent". The reviewer for *The Field* similarly decided that "he must have been a very uncomfortable man to live with". The *Times Literary Supplement* complained of a lack of explanation about how he wrote and that there was too much family detail.

The book commanded attention from some well-known authors including Howard Spring for *Country Life*, Sir Newman Flower for *The Sunday Times* and Graham Greene for *The New Statesman*. Greene recalled how enchanted he had been by reading Haggard's adventure stories when he was boy but astutely commented, "the hidden man was so imprisoned, when he does emerge it is against enormous pressure from the walls, and the effect is often one of horror, a risen Lazarus — next time he must be buried deeper".

Lilias finally gave up her "Countrywoman" columns; the story is that she drove up to Norwich to the EDP offices and forthrightly informed the editor that she was "all written out". She was succeeded by Adrian Bell, journalist, Suffolk farmer and author of the best-selling *Corduroy*. Agriculture was becoming a new industry: fields were enlarged and hedgerows cleared to gain every extra square foot of land for production. Pesticides and artificial fertilisers became the norm. It was a war on nature; the Waste Land was now. The Kinship in Husbandry, co-founded in 1941 by Rolfe Gardiner, H. J. Massingham and Gerald Wallop, the Earl of Portsmouth, and of which Adrian Bell was an early member, had promoted self-sufficiency and rural revival. Now a more scientific initiative in agriculture was needed; in 1943 Faber had published *The Living Soil* by Lady Eve Balfour which for the first time set out a scientific approach to a holistic view of the earth. Concerned about the effects of herbicides and intensive farming on animal and human health, Lady Eve had set up an experiment on two adjacent farms at Haughley Green, Suffolk, to observe food-chains through rotational cycles — one using fertilisers, herbicides and insecticides and one organic. It was the results of this experiment that formed the basis of the book which went to into nine editions and led directly to the establishment in 1946 of the Soil Association.

During the winter of 1953 there was heavy flooding along the north Norfolk coast. The sea breached the sea wall at Salthouse and Cley flooding Margaret's cottage. She had to retreat to the attic with a bull terrier under each arm and a bottle of scotch in one hand. She was there overnight and had to be rescued. That was the end of her home at "Hilldrop". For several years Margaret lived in the converted cowshed next to Lilias' Bath House until an inheritance enabled her to move to a house in twelve acres of land at Kettle Hill to the west of Blakeney. Lilias bought a cottage on an adjacent property. Reversing the arrangement that existed at Ditchingham, Margaret's house was substantial while Lilias' cottage, named Southdown, was tiny and lacking in pretension. However, the houses were almost unimportant compared to the breath-taking views of a vast westward stretch of coast as far as Holkham. Margaret began creating a new garden and planting a bluebell wood. Lilias often lent her cottage to

Southdown, Lilias' cottage near Kettle Hill at Blakeney. Courtesy Rosamund Woodton.

family members so that another generation of children could enjoy the open life and dreamy summer days along that magical coast line.

Together they spent their time bird-watching, taking picnics to the Point and enjoying a busy social life. Lilias was friendly with Rosamund Woodton of Blakeney whose father had farmed on the Spurrell estate at Newton St Faith. Margaret was a great friend of Jack Harrison, a Norfolk artist who lived at Hainford. Kathleen Ferrier's aunt lived at the bottom of the road. Mrs Marjorie Howell, a farmer's wife in Binham, helped Margaret for twenty-five years with food and cooking without any recompense which was often the old way of country families whose lives were entwined.

Lilias was able to indulge her love of travel again and also her pleasure in hot climates. She took some extensive cruises around the Mediterranean, often with Henta Scudamore, leaving her beloved dogs with Margaret; she sent back chatty letters and cards, often mentioning the dogs and sending kisses to them. She was

Margaret (in the boat) and Lilias on the beach, with some young relatives.
Cheyne Collection.

also able to visit Nada and Mark in Malta who were bringing up a family of four children. In 1956 Lilias revisited Rhodes, an island that she loved and the following year she and Henta rather adventurously drove over the Italian Alps and down into Yugoslavia where royalties from Rider's novels awaited them.

Margaret standing left, a boy relative, and Lilias with one of her dogs in the garden of the Bath House. Cheyne Collection.

At that time currency could not be sent out from Communist countries and Yugoslavia was something of an unknown quantity and not easy to negotiate. In 1958 she was in Brittany and the following year she and a group of friends toured France, Northern Italy and Greece and Rhodes again. In 1960 she tried Albania as well as Yugoslavia. During the mid-1950s, unshackled from the weekly commitment of a column, she wrote many features for the EDP about her travels, her domestic life, rural crafts, and any other matters that took her fancy from ghosts to raising children.

When the Cheynes returned to England in the early 1960s Angie transferred the whole estate to her nephew Mark who set about converting Ditchingham House into flats in an arrangement that remains to this day. Lilias and Angie each retained one for themselves. Mark and Nada and their four children settled at Ditchingham Lodge.

Another film of *King Solomon's Mines*, this time with George Montgomery, was released in 1959; there were also two radio adaptations in 1956 and 1966. Morton Cohen, an American professor from the University of New York City, wrote a biography, *Rider Haggard: His Life and Work*, and there was a flurry of interviews and publicity for Lilias when it was published in 1960. *She*, which had been translated into film many times, was released again in 1965 with Ursula Andress in the starring role.[23] All of this kept Rider's s reputation alive even though as an author he was now part of the old imperial past which the culture of the 1960s was abandoning as fast as it could. Yet, oddly in that climate, the film *Zulu* about Rorke's Drift, which made Michael Caine into an international film star, became a classic and spawned a tour industry all on its own.

Rider had one more surprise to offer up. C. J. Jung conceived of and contributed the first chapters to a popular and influential book called *Man and His Symbols* (London 1964) in which he cited Ayesha/She-Who-Must be-Obeyed as an illustration of the archetypal *"anima"* at work. Jung's writings in the post-war period energised and helped introduce New Age spirituality. To some degree Rider Haggard's work has shared in that mystique. It is worth noting that both men were influenced by the occult preoccupations of the *fin de siècle* and that New Age mysticism has some roots in Theosophy.[24]

At Jung's suggestion one of his disciples, Cornelia Brunner, began a ten-year study of the *"anima"* archetype in *King Solomon's Mines* and *She*.

Her work was published as *Anima as Fate* in 1963 and the following year Lilias invited Brunner and her husband to stay the night at Ditchingham House:

[23]   All citations from D. Whatmore's *H. Rider Haggard a Bibliography,* (London: 1987).

[24]   See Stephen Arata's references to "Imperial Gothic" in *Fictions of Loss in the Victorian Fin de Siècle,* 111 (Cambridge: CUP, 1996).

Lilias was very sympathetic with everything I had written about him in the book. That indicated to me how close she stood to her father, the complete opposite to her older sister.

> Rider Haggard had led a completely upright life. He did not dare to know well anyone except his lawful wife. He was so afraid of committing an indiscretion, that he once, when on a trip, barricaded his hotel room door with his suitcase for protection against a lady who had taken an interest in him. Such an attitude has the result that the man makes his daughter into the Anima.[25]
>
> … she [Lilias] had a lot of understanding for what I'd written about her father, for his fate, that through the grief for his son whom he'd lost so early, was in a way also linked to the sadness of his own unlived life. In his novels there is an unstilled longing for the "female soul", for the inner feminine complement, the "anima". He would only have been able to find it, if he had allowed himself to fall in love with other women. If he could have seen such falling in love as a projection of his own, still unconscious feminine side and been able to claim it back, he would have found his "wholeness". That was at his time — of which he was to an extent ahead — not yet possible. It is perhaps still very difficult for an Englishman who adheres to the gentleman-ideal and to the instruction of the church. Such emotional restrictions have as a consequence that the unstilled longing reaches out towards one's daughter and binds her to oneself.[26]

Brunner's book shows how Haggard learned and matured from his fictional creations which were much like dreams — *She* was written in a brief six weeks, pouring out of him with no let up.

Maureen Murdock's study of *Fathers' Daughters* suggests that while there are a wide variety of responses from daughters who overly identify with their fathers, "they commonly deny their own feelings" and that therefore their development of identity is "limited by the range of feelings her father allows her to experience".[27]

> A father's daughter is groomed to be like her father ("You're like me"), yet she must be sure to remain less powerful. The unspoken agreement is that she will remain loyal to him, which means upholding his values and standards… The covenant with her father prevents her from forming deep relationships with

---

[25]   Letter from Cornelia Brunner to the author, September 30th 1992.
[26]   Letter to the author from Cornelia Brunner, January 27th 1993.
[27]   *Fathers' Daughters: Breaking the Ties That Bind,* New Orleans: 1994, 34/35.

either men or women or from achieving true autonomy.[28]

Another Jungian, Marie-Louise von Franz, took a rather broader view when she wrote:

> Why one girl is more influenced by the father's anima and
> another by the mother's animus depends, I think, on the
> original disposition of the child. One child will develop a
> strong father complex and the other, of the same family, does
> not. It is the effect of the inborn disposition that this daughter
> is more concentrated on the father and more affected by the
> unconscious.

That Lilias began writing a book about her mother's family indicates that she was ready to claim back her maternal ancestors. She had already dipped into the material for some of her columns and now she wrote the full story. *Too Late for Tears* is an exceptionally interesting book in terms of social manners and local history between 1830 and 1860; Lilias put together the patchwork of diary entries and letters to create a beautifully written, if slight, volume. What becomes clear is that the Margitsons and their connections, the Hamiltons, Hartcups and Hildyards, were just as much part of the wide web of "gentle" or upper middle class Norfolk families as the Haggards; they just didn't make so much noise. While the tragic childhood deaths of her aunts, uncles and brothers and then of her parents left Louie (Louisa) sadly orphaned, she was still very close to her Hartcup cousins who lived in Bungay and she was completely at home in Ditchingham.

The tragedy of successive childhood deaths at Ditchingham House was from the infected water from a household well that was too close to the drains which had cracked, and from a tubercular nursery maid. In addition three babies died almost as soon as they were born — from what cause is not known but infant mortality rates were high in all classes. The damp and the cold were constant enemies and everyone was always getting colds, chills, influenza and sickness. Marianna Louisa Margitson was, in the end, the sole heiress. As Lilias pointed out, against all the genetic and environmental odds, Louie was physically and mentally robust.

Too Late for Tears is a wonderful portrait of three sisters growing up in the early Victorian period and displaying manners and attitudes that we recognise from Jane Austen. Religion played an overpowering role in their lives, as did duty and obedience. The book is redolent with a sense of loss but in the end Lilias offers hope in the new generations of children that have played in the gardens of Ditchingham. Family life — extended family life in the case of the Haggards

[28]   Ibid, 60.

Lilias with one of her dogs beside the Waveney. Cheyne Collection.

— is the core of renewal: it is a conservative resurrection and follows the great importance her father gave to family genealogy and dynasty.

During the Christmas period of 1967 there were many guests and relatives staying in the various houses at Ditchingham so Lilias went to stay at All Hallows Convent for the duration. While she was there she picked up an influenza virus from the cook so that when she came home to her flat in Ditchingham House she was quite ill. Margaret Spurrell was staying with her. They had adjacent bedrooms and would call to each other over early morning cups of tea. On the morning of January 9th 1968 Margaret heard a great crash as Lilias' tea tray hit the floor. She hurried into her room to find that Lilias had had a massive heart attack from which she had died instantly. An autopsy report showed that her heart, which was enlarged as a result of the rheumatic fever of her teenage years, had literally burst.

By her own request her ashes were buried in Ditchingham churchyard next to Jock's grave.

Too Late for Tears was published posthumously.

Epilogue

As well as the formal obituaries of Lilias which appeared in the press, there was a personal one in the February 1968 *Ditchingham Parish Newsletter* — a monthly sheet which she had helped originate and to which she had contributed regularly during the last decade. The vicar, the Reverend Ken Lewis, noted that he had first read *I Walked By Night* when he had joined the Royal Tank Regiment before the war and was stationed at Warminster. It had the effect on him, to which R.H. Mottram had alluded, of resonating with all his own images and feelings about Norfolk and the country he valued and for which he would be fighting. Lewis added several very important comments on Lilias' character which he had had ample time to observe at parish meetings. One was that Lilias never took herself too seriously, the second was that in coming to decisions she always took the long view, third, that, unlike many people, she said what she meant and last, that her faith was "sound, simple and direct".

She expressed that peculiarly English mixture of Christianity and pantheism:

> It is not given to all men and women to comprehend the mystery
> of that night of terror when the full moon of the Passover had
> set and Mary Magdalene entered the garden and stood before
> the sepulchre, to see in the first glory of the risen son that figure
> of terrifying beauty before an empty tomb — and heard those
> astounding words: "He is not here — He is risen."

> But the gardener holding the packet of tiny seeds knows that
> in his hand a whole garden lies asleep. In the transparency of
> an unfolding leaf, in the opening of the perfect flower within
> the bud, in the bird brooding her speckled eggs, in the whole
> loveliness and promise of spring, lie man's festival of joy and
> hope of immortality. A joy often forgotten in this sad old world
> with its anxieties and dogmas, its doubts and scientific quibbles.
> A joy which I think Robert Louis Stevenson had in mind when
> he wrote a prayer for the use of his household, both white and
> coloured [sic], in Samoa.

"Look down upon Thy servants with a patient eye, even as
Thou sendest sun and rain; look down, call upon the dry bones;
quicken, enliven; re-create in us the soul of service, the spirit of
peace; renewing in us the sense of joy."[1]

In a century in which the political Left and political Right sought social
utopias, Lilias found nature itself a source of revelation.   While diaspora of all
kinds were taking place she was a steady and diligent champion of the benefits of
identification with place. That her writing was grounded in the local is central to
its importance.

In England the landscape created by the social structure of the squirearchy was
broken up after the war by the wholesale destruction of the great country houses
along with the grand vistas, the home farms and the estate and independent
villages that went with them. Gradually villages have often become little more
than dormitories for local towns.

1963 saw the landmark publication of Rachel Carson's *Silent Spring* which
effectively drew attention to the devastation caused by the spraying of crops with
DDT in the United States. But it did much more than that: it was a *réveille* to
western countries about the impact and state of agri-business:

> ... from *Silent Spring* onwards environmental awareness began
> to grow. This was not primarily in the form of an organised
> "green" politics but rather in a generalised sense that something
> was going wrong with agriculture and the countryside ... from
> the mid-1960s onwards there were real concerns which could
> not be dismissed as simple golden ageism. The most striking
> of these, because it was visually so powerful, was the loss of
> the hedgerows. Between 1946 and 1974 farmers removed a
> quarter of the hedgerows in England and Wales — some 120,000
> miles in all. In some areas it was worse; in Norfolk 45 per cent
> of hedgerows were removed in the same period, mainly for
> increased barley production, and in Cambridgeshire 40 per cent
> were removed.[2]

The effect of this change was not just aesthetic but meant the loss of flora and
fauna on a massive scale. Wildflowers, small animals, insects, whole species of

1   LRH, *A Country Scrapbook*, 231.
2   Statistics from Marion Shoard *The Theft of the Countryside* (London: 1980) 34 –
     41 quoted by Alun Howkins in *The Death of Rural England* (London: Routledge
     2003, 196).

birds were significantly reduced or wiped out – and what no one at the Ministry of Agriculture seems ever to have thought about – the bees which pollinate the crops were decimated. What was becoming clear – to those people who thought about it at all – was that farmers had ceased to be custodians of the countryside.

In East Anglia the dying skills and crafts of rural life were collected up in a series of books by George Ewart Evans, most famous of which was *Ask the Fellows Who Cut the Hay* (1955) while rural cultural history was expressed most lovingly and lyrically by Ronald Blythe in *Akenfield* (1969).

There was a new wave of interest in food production and some of the original promoters such as Rolfe Gardiner lived to see a revival of Organicism. There was also a reaction to urban life and a new back-to-the-land movement spearheaded by the writings of John Seymour – *Farming for Self-Sufficiency: Independence on a 5-Acre Farm* (1973). With the spiritual revelation associated with the New Age of Aquarius came experiments in communal living such as the Findhorn community in Scotland which developed a totally holistic view of the earth, nature and what it means to be human on this planet.

During the years that ushered in the millennium a new style of country writing emerged which does not rely on those patterns of agriculture or rural culture which have long gone. The leading names in this genre include the Essex writer J.A. Baker with his much-lauded study of *The Peregrine* (1969) a book that combined acute observation with literary style. The late Roger Deakin was a writer and environmentalist who settled in Suffolk. He co-founded an organisation called Common Ground which aimed to recognise, understand and preserve ordinary places – not just the outstanding landscapes preserved by the National Trust. He is famous for his two books *Waterlog* (1999) about "wild swimming" and *Wildwood* (2007), published posthumously about human relationships to trees. Richard Mabey, a writer who settled in Norfolk, wrote the highly successful *Food for Free* (1972) which drew attention to all the edible plants that we ignore in our rush towards supermarket food. Later he turned to the therapeutic value of relating to the natural world in *Nature Cure* (2005). This was a theme that Lilias had emphasised time and again. Mark Cocker, a Norfolk naturalist, is best known for his books on birds and culture: *Birds Britannica* (2005) and *Crow Country* (2007). The decline of bird life is recognised as emblematic of all that is wrong with our exploitation of nature. Robert Macfarlane, a travel writer and broadcaster, explores what is left of "wild" landscapes. Robert Pogue Harrison, a Stanford professor of philosophy, brings a deep consideration to matters of human relationship to culture and the natural world, especially gardens.

All this new, original and inspiring country writing is best summed up by William Bloom, the holistic author and educator:

The appreciation of nature brings the environmental campaigner into alliance with the lyrical lovers of landscape, and with the animist tribal religions and pagans and feminists, who honour every aspect of the planet as being sacred and alive.[3]

This view of nature as a fundamental spiritual source is a flame that spluttered in the mid twentieth century and Lilias was among those few who kept it alight.

[3]   William Bloom, introduction to the chapters on Gaia from *The Penguin Book of New Age and Holistic Writing*, edited by William Bloom (London: the Penguin Press, 2000), 97.

Bibliography

Arata, Stephen.   *Fictions of Loss in the Victorian Fin de Siècle*, Cambridge: CUP, 1996.

Ardis, Ann and Lewis, Leslie W. (Editors) *Women's Experience of Modernity 1875-1945*, Baltimore: John Hopkins University Press, 2003.

Athill, Diana.   *Life Class*, London: Granta, 2002.

Bishop, Peter   *An Archetypal Constable. National Identity and the geography of Nostalgia*. London: Athlone, 1995.

Blythe, Ronald   *Field Work. A Selection of Essays*. Norwich: Black Dog Books, 2007.

Butler, J.R.M.   *Lord Lothian (Philip Kerr. 1882-1940*. London: Macmillan & Co Ltd, 1960.

Brunner, Cornelia   *Anima As Fate*. Dallas, Texas: Spring Publications, Inc, 1986. First published in German in Zurich, 1963.

Coan, Stephen. (Editor)   *Diary of an African Journey* Pietermaritzburg: University of Natal Press; 2000.

Cohen, Morton   *Rider Haggard — His Life and Works*. London: Hutchinson, 1960.

Coupe, Laurence.   *Myth*. London: Routledge, 1997.

Ellis, Peter Beresford   *H. Rider Haggard: A Voice from the Infinite*. London: Routledge, Kegan Paul, 1978

Farson, Daniel.   *Henry, An Appreciation of Henry Williamson*, London: Michael Joseph, 1982.

Fitzgerald, Penelope   *Charlotte Mew and Her Friends.* London: Collins, 1984.

Fraser, Robert   *Victorian Quest Romance* Plymouth: Northcote House, 1998.

Goodman, Jean   *Edward Seago: A Wider Canvas,* Banham, Erskine Press; 2002.

Gottlieb, Julie V.   *Feminine Fascism. Women in Britain's Fascist Movement.* London and New York : I.B. Tauris, 2000.

Graf, Fritz   *Greek Mythology. An Introduction*. Baltimore and London: John Hopkins University Press; 1993.

Granzow, Brigitt   *A Mirror of Nazism. British opinion and the Emergence of Hitler 1929-1933*. London: Victor Gollancz Ltd, 1964.

Griffiths, Richard   *Fellow Travellers of the Right. British Enthusiasts for Nazi Germany 1933-9.* London: Constable, 1980.

Haggard, Lilias Rider   *I Walked by Night*. London: Ivor Nicholson & Watson Ltd, 1935. *The Rabbit Skin Cap*. London: Collins, 1939. *Norfolk Life*. London: Faber & Faber, 1943. *Norfolk Notebook*. London: Faber & Faber, 1946. *Country Scrapbook*. London: Faber & Faber, 1950. *The Cloak that I Left*. London: Hodder & Stoughton, 1951. *Too Late for Tears*. Bungay, Suffolk: Waveney Publications, 1968.

Haggard, H. Rider   *A Farmer's Year*. London: Longmans, Green, and Co, 1899. *A Gardener's Year*. London: Longmans, Green, and Co, 1905. *She*. London: Longmans, Green, and Co, 1887. *When the World Shook*. London: Cassell and Co Ltd, 1919.

The Days of My Life. 2 vols London: Longman, 1926.

Hayman, Ronald.   *A Life of Jung.* London: Bloomsbury, 1999.

Haymon, Sylvia   *The Quivering Tree. An East Anglian Childhood.* London: Constable, 1990.

Heller, Thomas C., Morton Sosna, and Wellbery, David E. (Editors). *Reconstructing Individualism.* Stanford CA: Stanford University Press, 1986.

Higgins, D.S.   *The Private Diaries of Sir Henry Rider Haggard 1914-1925.* London: Cassell, 1980.

Higgins, D.S.   *Rider Haggard: The Great Storyteller.* London: Cassell, 1981.

Howkins, Alun   *The Death of Rural England,* London: Routledge, 2003.

Ingman, Heather   *Women's Fiction Between the Wars. Mothers, Daughters and Writing.* Edinburgh: Edinburgh, 1998.

Jaffe, Aniela   *The Myth of Meaning: Jung and the Expansion of Consciousness.* New York: Penguin, 1975. First published 1971.

Johnson, Mark   *The Body in the Mind.* Chicago: University of Chicago Press, 1974.

Jung, Carl J.   *Jung on Synchronicity and the Paranormal. Key Readings selected and introduced by Roderick Main.* London: Routledge, 1977.

Jung, Carl J.   *Aspects of the Feminine.* London: Routledge, 1982.

Jung, Carl J.   *Aspects of the Masculine.* London: Routledge, 1989.

Jung, Carl J. (Editor)   *Man and His Symbols.* London: Aldus, 1964.

Light, Alison   *Forever England. Femininity, Literature and Conservatism Between the Wars.* London: Routledge, 1991.

Macfarlane, Robert   *The Wild Places.* London: Granta Books, 2007.

Manthorpe, Victoria   *Children of the Empire. The Victorian Haggards.* London: Gollancz, 1996

Massingham, H. J.   *Remembrance.* London: Batsford, 1941.

Massingham, H.J.   *The Faith of a Fieldsman.* London: Museum Press Ltd, 1951.

Matless, David   *Landscape and Englishness,* London: Reaktion Books Ltd, 1998.

Mitchell, Juliet and Rose, Jacqueline. (Editors) *Feminine Sexuality: Jacques Lacan and the École Freudienne.* Translated by Jacqueline Rose. London: Macmillan, 1982.

Montifiore, Janet.   *Men and Women Writers of the 1930s.* London and New York: Routledge 1996.

Murdock, Maureen.   *Fathers' Daughters: Breaking the Ties That Bind.* New Orleans: Spring Journal Books 1994.

Nicholson, Virginia   *Singled Out.* London: Viking 2007.

Pakenham, Thomas.   *The Scramble for Africa* London: Weidenfeld &Nicolson, 1991.

Shepherd, June   *Doreen Wallace 1897-1989, Writer and Social Campaigner.* Lewiston, New York, EMP, 2000.

Wade Martins, Susanna   *The Countryside of East Anglia, Changing Landscapes 1870-1950* Woodbridge, The Boydell Press, 2008.

Wainwright, Martin. (Editor) *Wartime Country Diaries.* London: Guardianbooks, 2007.

Warner, Val   *Charlotte Mew Collected Poems and Prose.* Manchester: Carcanet Press, 1981.

Wehr, Demaris S.   *Jung and Feminism: Liberating Archetypes.* London: Routledge, 1988.

Whatmore, D.E.   *H. Rider Haggard — A Bibliography.* London: Mansell, 1987.

Woodman, Marion.   *The Pregnant Virgin,* Toronto: Inner City Books, 1985.

Index

Holtby, Winifred 126, 149

India 17, 49
Isandlwana 171
Isis 38, 44, 84, 88

Jackson, Frederick 35
Jackson, Lilly 34
Jebb, Gladwyn 20
Jung, Carl 38, 95, 177, 185, 187

Kessingland 33
King Solomon's Mines 19, 174, 177
Kipling, John, 'Jack' 55, 57
Kipling, Rudyard 55, 57, 78, 81, 93, 120,
    128, 129
Kitchener, Lord Herbert 17, 57
kitchen garden 23
knighthood, Rider Haggard 49

Landau, Rom 124
Lawrence, Margery 126
Lewis, Reverend Ken 181
Liberal Unionist Party 45
Light, Alison 78
Lloyd George, David 44
Longman, Freddie 51
Longmans 48
Longrigg, John 107
Lowther, Miss 89, 91
Lyndhurst, Bill 79

Mabey, Richard 183
Macfarlane, Robert 183
Madame Tussaud's 29
Mann, Ethel 105
Margitson, Louisa, *see* Haggard, Mariana
    Louisa
Massingham, H.J. 104, 165, 174, 186
Matless, David 98, 128, 136, 137, 148
May Balls 48
Meade, Helena 84
Mettingham 76-77, 79, 94
Mexico, Mexico City 19, 22

Morden Grange Auxiliary Hospital 68, 70
Morton, H.V. 101
Mosley, Oswald 123, 129
Mottram, R.H. 11, 168, 181
Murdock, Maureen 93, 95-88, 178
Museum, South Kensington 29

New Zealand 57
Norfolk Record Office 37
Norwich Castle Museum 67, 114

officer class 92
Oxford Street 66

Page, Doris 62-63, 79
Paine, Thomas 18,113
Passchendaele, battle of 68, 132, 185, 188
Paton, Charlotte 114
Perry, Gerty 101-94
Perry, Jimmy 101
Porteous, Crichton 104
Positivism 17
preservation 97, 106, 142, 160

Quatermain, Allan 19,

Red Cross 56, 59-60, 65, 68, 79, 138
Red House 76
reincarnation 83-76, 172
rheumatic fever 38
Robbins, Olive 45
Robinson, W. Fothergill 59
Rolfe, Frederick 32, 107-108, 110-114,
    143, 174, 183
Romanovs 76
Roosevelt, Theodore 45, 76
Rorke's Drift 171, 177
Ross, Sir Ronald 80
Rotenberg, Helena 83
Royal Commission on Coastal Erosion 46

Sackville-West, Vita 148
Samuel, Evelyn 89-82
Sawbridge, Margaret 166

Lightning Source UK Ltd.
Milton Keynes UK
UKOW06f1802161215

264869UK00003B/113/P

9 781909 796188